THE ACT OF
LEADERSHIP

'Warm, witty but, above all, wise. This book is an essential companion for any leader.'

Damian Hughes, visiting Professor of Organisational Psychology and Change, author and co-host of _The High Performance Podcast_

'Sometimes it takes someone to simplify the chaos, to not just open one's eyes, but open one's mind as well. In a world ever changing, and ever challenging, Dan Haesler not only inspires you to be the best version of yourself, but provides the space and steps to become that for yourself and your team — especially if you think you're at the top of your game!'

Anna Meares OAM, Dual Olympic Champion

'Haesler provides a no-nonsense, plain talking guide to modern leadership that draws from the best and most current sources in psychology and management sciences. Whether seeking to build new skills, tune up old ones, or just searching for a dose of inspiration, this is a book both managers and leadership coaches will deeply appreciate.'

Professor Richard M Ryan, Australian Catholic University, co-founder of Self-Determination Theory

THE ACT OF LEADERSHIP

A playbook for leading with humility, clarity and purpose.

DAN HAESLER

WILEY

First published in 2021 by John Wiley & Sons Australia, Ltd
42 McDougall St, Milton Qld 4064
Office also in Melbourne

Typeset in ITC Cheltenham Std 10.5pt/14.5pt

ISBN: 978-0-730-39211-8

A catalogue record for this book is available from the National Library of Australia

Cover design by Wiley
Front Cover Images: © Twins Design Studio/Shutterstock, © MicroOne/Shutterstock, © Ron Dale/Shutterstock

Disclaimer
The material in this publication is of the nature of general comment only, and does not represent professional advice. It is not intended to provide specific guidance for particular circumstances and it should not be relied on as the basis for any decision to take action or not take action on any matter which it covers. Readers should obtain professional advice where appropriate, before making any such decision. To the maximum extent permitted by law, the author and publisher disclaim all responsibility and liability to any person, arising directly or indirectly from any person taking or not taking action based on the information in this publication.

CONTENTS

ABOUT THE AUTHOR

Dan Haesler is a coach whose work focuses on creating happier, healthier and higher performance. He works with people in order to help them, and the people around them, to thrive, professionally and personally.

Dan's clients include elite athletes and Olympians, as well as corporate and educational leaders.

As a Director of Cut Through Coaching, he is also an international keynote speaker and regularly presents alongside industry leaders, Olympians, Oscar winners and even His Holiness the Dalai Lama on topics of leadership, mindset, motivation and peak performance.

Before moving to Australia, Dan was also once identified, on national TV, as the UK's worst housemate.

Having improved (most of) his domestic habits, Dan now lives in Sydney with Samira, their two children, and a beagle called Mr Pickles.

His website is www.danhaesler.com

He'd love to connect with you on Twitter or Instagram at @danhaesler.

Or if you prefer your social media a little more professional, you can also find Dan on LinkedIn.

INTRODUCTION

If I were to ask you what a good leader looks like—what they do and how they make you feel—you could probably tell me. Hopefully, you could name one or two from your own experience in the workplace.

And, if I asked you what a poor leader looks like—what they do, how they make you feel—again, you could tell me. You might be able to name one or two or three. You might even have nicknames for them, and you certainly have stories about them that you tell at dinner parties to try to one-up your friends about who has the worst boss.

So why is it that in the cold light of day—perhaps when you're perusing the business section of a bookstore—you're quite clear on what good leadership is, but in the heat of the day-to-day running of your team, you sometimes act more like the leader people talk about at dinner parties?

As I see it, there are three main reasons for this, two more easily addressed than the other one:

- *Reason #1:* You're human. (This is the one that's not as easy to address but we'll give it a go in part I of this book.)

- *Reason #2:* The way you've learned about leadership. (We'll address this in parts II and III.)

- *Reason #3:* You don't do the things you've learned. (This book is aimed at helping you to take what you've learned and use it to form new habits and—where necessary—break old ones.)

A few years ago, I was contracted by the National Rugby League (NRL) in Australia to present workshops to teams across the competition. My workshop was aimed at exploring the leadership links between mindset, habits and performance. It was deliberately designed so that players, coaches, the backroom staff and players' partners could relate to it either on a professional or personal level.

A couple of days after presenting to the playing group at one club, my phone rang. It was the club's welfare officer telling me how the senior players in particular had loved it, and that the captain of the club—a State of Origin representative—was insistent that the club engage me over the course of the upcoming season. In the skipper's words, what I had presented was 'the missing link', and now the welfare officer was telling me, 'Mate, we want you to ourselves. Not only is this stuff good for them as people, the boys think this will give them the competitive edge over the rest of the comp. Mate, we want to put you in one of our jerseys!'

I was buzzing.

However, the head coach—who didn't take part in my session— wanted to meet me to get a better idea of what a long-term engagement might look like. As with most NRL clubs, the head coach is the one whose opinion really matters, and I was excited as I drove to the club's headquarters because I'd heard this coach was a good guy, and, given the captain and senior players were keen to get going, I felt this meeting could only go well.

I set about explaining some of my approaches, and the rationale behind them—as I'll do in this book—and why any group of people striving towards a common aim might benefit from adopting them. The club's director of football, a highly regarded member of the rugby league community, was also in the meeting and I was pleased to see him nodding along enthusiastically as I made my pitch. 'How well is this going ...', I thought to myself.

Not that well, as it turned out.

My pitch did nothing to convince the coach that his captain, senior players or the welfare officer were on the right track. As he told me politely, 'Yeah, I know all this, and besides, we already have someone come in once every couple of months or so to do this stuff with us'.

That was essentially all he said, and it was clearly the conclusion of the meeting.

I left somewhat deflated, and it was no surprise when, a day or so later, the club's welfare officer contacted me to confirm what I already knew. The club wouldn't be pursuing the engagement.

I found myself reflecting on two things in particular over the ensuing days:

- Had I been too confident walking into that meeting?

- Was I less than fully prepared?

Yes, and yes. Not a great combination.

I had assumed that because the senior players and the captain were championing my work, the coach would recognise the obvious benefit to having me on board.

I was annoyed because I pride myself on my preparation and attention to detail, so to walk out of this meeting knowing that I hadn't prepared for anything other than a positive outcome rankled me somewhat.

But I was also left reflecting on what the coach had said.

He had told me he knew it all and that they do this stuff every couple of months with someone from outside the club.

Now, this isn't meant to sound like sour grapes, but he was illustrating the three reasons for poor leadership that I highlighted above:

- *Reason #1:* He's human. As a human, his confidence in knowing everything perhaps blinded him to the effectiveness or otherwise of what they were currently doing.

- *Reason #2:* The way he'd learned about leadership. The manner in which they 'did this stuff'—once every couple of months or so—spoke to how he viewed learning as an event, and only when an external consultant came in.

- *Reason #3:* He doesn't do what he *has* learned. The coach would have learned that it's important to listen to his people, but clearly he wasn't doing that because he seemed oblivious to the fact that his players and back-room staff clearly didn't feel they were 'doing' it anyway.

Leadership isn't something you know. It's something you show. All the time.

Had I been better prepared for our meeting, I might have been able to articulate these counterpoints in a respectful way.

But I wasn't. So I didn't.

Six months later the coach left the club amid claims he had 'lost the playing group'.

Obviously, I can't say that if I'd been engaged by the club things would have been different. There would have been numerous complex issues at play. But in the years since that meeting with the coach, I've spent many hours working with all kinds of leaders from all walks of life, and I've had the opportunity to reflect on some of the reasons people don't quite have a handle on what it means to lead their people.

I've researched the common challenges that leaders deal with as well as the theories that explain why these challenges arise. And crucially, I've worked side-by-side with leaders and their teams as they've applied these theories to enhance how they live and work. I've also had the chance to dive deeper into these theories with some of the world's prominent leadership thinkers for my podcast, *Habits of Leadership*.

So I'm now offering the world another leadership book.

To be honest, I'm not even sure the world needs another leadership book. I said as much to the publishers in our earliest conversations, and then realised that's probably not the way to go, so I quickly changed tack.

In the traditional sense, this isn't another leadership book. Most books delve into one or two concepts, while this book seeks to cover a lot of ground in a short amount of time. It's a playbook of sorts for busy leaders with an emphasis on helping them create new habits and ways of being in their day-to-day leadership that they can enact almost immediately.

Here's a rundown of what you'll gain from reading this book.

Part I tackles the 'you' stuff and asks you to reflect on 'How do I show up?' We'll explore some of the challenges you face as a leader purely because you're human:

- *Chapter 1* — 'Is this book for you: what kind of leader do you want to be?' We'll look at some of the common archetypes used to describe leaders and leadership. You'll be challenged to reflect on which — if any — apply to you, and then I'll suggest some of the key takeaways each archetype might get from the book.

- *Chapter 2*—'Be mindful, not mindless: the importance of being in the moment'. We'll explore some of the fundamental human behaviours and responses that govern our day-to-day experiences. You'll be encouraged to consider mindfulness as the act of being deliberate and intentional. As much as we'll discuss breathing techniques, we'll keep circling back to the notion of acting mindfully as opposed to mindlessly.

- *Chapter 3*—'Assume nothing: the biases that stop you from seeing what's really there'. We'll look at some of the common cognitive biases that affect how we view ourselves and our impact on others and address recency bias, blind spot bias and the Dunning–Kruger effect. My goal in this chapter is to encourage you to rethink how you think.

- *Chapter 4*—'How to turn it around: why you don't learn from your mistakes'. We'll address mindset and how it affects behaviours, particularly around changing your behaviour as a result of a setback. This chapter serves to set up parts II and III of the book by encouraging you to adopt a mindset that will allow you to get the most out of the subsequent chapters.

Part II addresses the 'you and them' stuff with a particular focus on creating and nurturing environments in which you and your team do your best work:

- *Chapter 5*—'Mum was wrong: it really *does* matter what others think of you'. We'll seek to address why 360 feedback surveys rarely have the impact they should. As well as making the case that the best people to determine whether or not you're an effective leader are the people you lead, you'll be presented with a practical and attractive way to engage more of your team in your leadership development.

- *Chapter 6*—'Make it safe to stuff up: high performance is not about being perfect'. We'll help you understand the essential—and often missing—ingredient needed for teams to be high performing. This chapter will help you create a culture where risk-taking is welcome, and where there is permission for candour that allows all voices to be heard and valued, particularly when those voices are saying something you might otherwise not want to hear. Yes, you read that right.

- *Chapter 7*—'Less carrot, less stick: find out what makes people tick'. We'll delve into the world of motivation and explore how leaders can empower the people they lead to authentically engage in their work.

- *Chapter 8*—'Be better at change: stop trying to get people on the bus'. Exploring why attempts at individual and organisational change fail, and how you can avoid the common roadblocks, we'll tackle the issue of employee engagement through the lens of organisational change.

- *Chapter 9*—'Less is more: create space so your team can step up'. We'll seek to help you become more coach-like and empower you to empower your teams. This chapter will show you how to adopt more coach-like techniques in your every day interactions, rather than just viewing coaching as an event.

Part III addresses the tactical stuff and provides advice for dealing with some of the most common challenges you might face on a day-to-day basis in your role as a leader:

- *Chapter 10*—'Stop wasting people's time: running meetings that matter'. We'll discuss how to run better meetings so you actually get stuff done. Nuff said.

- *Chapter 11*—'No more sh!t sandwiches: have better 1:1s with your team'. We'll explore why most of the feedback we're given doesn't have the cut-through the feedback giver was hoping for. Ever since school we've ignored or made excuses as to why we don't need to take on feedback. This chapter challenges the common wisdom around the popular Positive—Constructive (or Negative)—Positive approach to giving feedback (because it's wrong) and introduces you to the SHIFT model for conversations. This tried and tested model can be deployed in virtually any setting and enacts all the theory of the previous 10 chapters.

- *Chapter 12*—'Have less difficult conversations: start having adult ones instead'. We'll tackle one of the most common challenges we see for leaders: the art of having difficult conversations. The two main reasons people don't like these are that they 'don't like confrontation', or they 'don't want to risk the relationship'. This chapter will demonstrate that even conversations that are related to poor performance need not be confrontational and can indeed build relationships. It will give you the skills to empower people to take more ownership of their work.

- *Conclusion*—'Roger Federer still feels the need for a coach, and you don't? Seriously?' We'll encourage leaders to reflect on the fact that change is hard, and even the best in the world in their field usually have some form of coach. For those leaders not keen to engage with a coach, I provide a reflection and action journal to help leaders identify their growth opportunities and then self-regulate in their attempts to embed their learning from the book in their own context.

Each chapter is intended to serve as a coaching session that identifies a prevalent leadership challenge and explores the research, theories and concepts to help you address it.

You'll be encouraged to reflect on what each chapter means for you personally and for your team by using my coaching lens of developing insights, intentions and actions. Too often we might only develop one or two of the three necessary elements to effect positive change. Figure I.1 identifies how each of the three elements of coaching interplay.

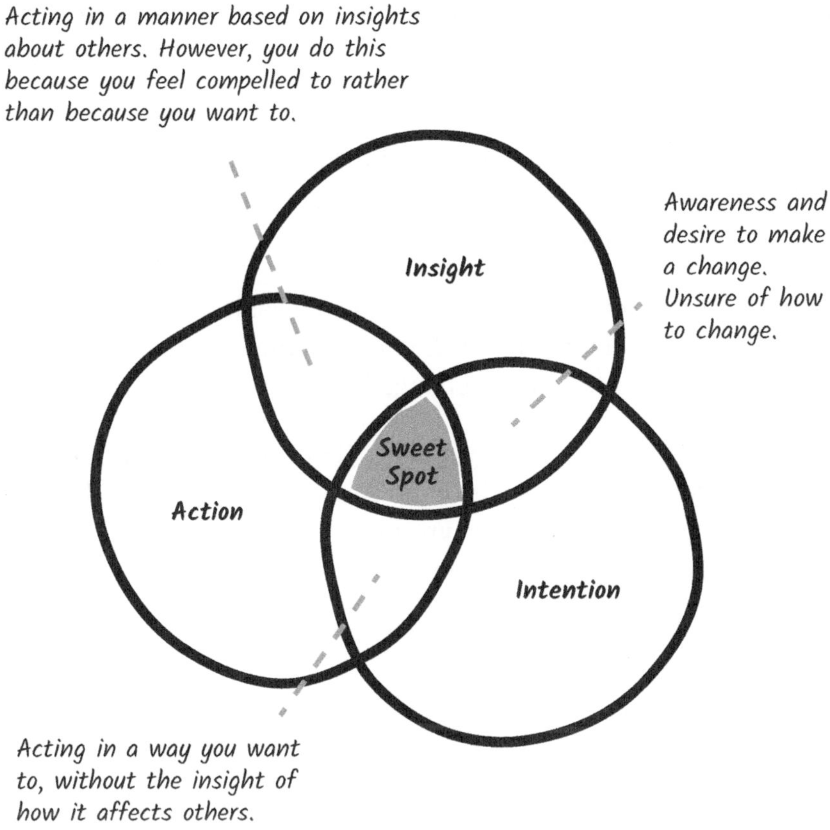

Acting in a manner based on insights about others. However, you do this because you feel compelled to rather than because you want to.

Awareness and desire to make a change. Unsure of how to change.

Insight

Sweet Spot

Action

Intention

Acting in a way you want to, without the insight of how it affects others.

Figure I.1: the sweet spot of coaching

The sweet spot of coaching is where we use insights to motivate ourselves to act in a new way that—as well as improving performance—provides us with new insights. You'll be asked to reflect on the sweet spot at the end of each chapter.

Importantly, each chapter also presents an Act of Leadership where I'll share with you some strategies and techniques, and, in some cases, even words to say in order for you to enhance your leadership to address the challenges you've identified.

For those readers who want to dig deeper into specific concepts, this book serves as a gateway to other books written by world-leading authorities in their field. I've been fortunate to chat with the authors of some of these books and so I am able to add further insights as to how their thinking informs the practical strategies I use every day with clients.

You can also access tools, further resources and full podcast interviews with the people mentioned in the book at www.actofleadership.com.

With the exception of the publicly recognisable identities in this book, the names and nature of the organisations of the people I use in the case studies have been changed in the interests of privacy.

Had I written this book three years ago, I might have left a copy with the coach for him to flick through. And maybe—just maybe—he might not have lost the playing group.

Or his job.

Part I

THE 'YOU' STUFF

Let's explore some of the challenges you face as a leader purely because you're human.

Chapter 1

IS THIS BOOK FOR YOU?

What kind of leader do you want to be?

This chapter in a nutshell

- you'll be introduced to the prominent thinking around leadership theories and styles

- you'll be encouraged to reflect on how these theories and styles inform your own leadership

- you'll see how each chapter of this book might help you enhance your leadership

Why this book? Why not the one sitting beside it in the store?

Maybe it was given to you as a gift and you're still trying to figure out whether or not to invest your time in it.

I get it. You're busy and you don't want to waste time reading a book that isn't for you.

This chapter aims to help you ascertain whether or not this book can help you, and how it might be able to help you. You will chart a course that might mean you flick through some chapters quicker than others, or you might choose to focus on just one or two.

In essence, I'm trying to write in a similar manner to how I coach. Not everyone needs everything, and some people only need one thing.

Rather than tell you something, let me start by asking you something:

What kind of leader do you want to be?

Take some time to ponder and then note down what comes to mind for you.

....

....

....

....

Look back over what you wrote and consider:

- Was it easy to answer that question? Were you surprised by how much space I gave you to write in? Did you need more or less space?

4

- Did you focus on your ability to deliver results based on products, processes, policies or people?

- Did you compare yourself to others? Are they well-known leaders or people only you would know?

- Does anything you wrote surprise you?

- Have you ever taken time to consider this question before? Where have you gone looking for answers? Have you looked for a mentor or just taken your lead from what you think the organisation expects?

- How satisfied are you with your leadership right now? If you had to score yourself out of 10 as a leader, what would you say? How inclined are you to want to improve?

By the way, if you scored yourself a 10, this is either not the book for you or (more likely) absolutely the book for you, and I'm guessing perhaps it was given to you as a 'gift'.

Now, unlike at school when teachers used to lie and tell you, 'There are no right or wrong answers', when it comes to these questions—and, in fact, any questions I ask as a coach—we're not as interested in the notion of right and wrong as we are in what it brings up for you. What new awareness can we create from asking questions of ourselves and each other? Coaching, and this book, is not a test. Your answers and thoughts are yours alone, and a piece of paper can't judge, criticise or hold anything against you, so whenever I ask you to reflect, the more open and honest you can be with yourself, the more awareness you'll create.

Are you up for that? If so, this might be the book for you.

But back to that question, 'What kind of leader do you want to be?'

In my experience, some people struggle to answer the question because they haven't spent enough time thinking about leadership and what it really means to be a leader.

In many cases, people find themselves in a position of leadership by default or as a result of being the last one standing, or in some cases being tapped on the shoulder and given an opportunity. I've lost count of the number of people I've worked with who say, 'I never set out for this', or 'I've never thought of myself as a leader'. Sometimes this is an indication of their humility, but more often than not it's also a sign that they've unexpectedly found themselves in a position of leadership and they're still trying to figure out whether they're really the right person for the job.

Impostor syndrome is quite common among leaders. But fear not, as the host of *Coaching for Leaders*, Dave Stachowiak says, 'Leaders aren't born. They're made'. With a little reflection and deliberate action, you can become a great leader.

When working with a leader for the first time, rather than jumping straight into what needs to be fixed or improved, I've found it useful to spend time exploring the concept of leadership with them, and I'd like to do that now with you.

So, what makes a good leader?

Several well-established theories and styles form our understanding of leadership and what good leadership looks like. While I won't cover them all here, it might be helpful to dig into some of the more prominent ones at this point.

For a time, it was thought that leadership was something that either came naturally or didn't. You were either a natural leader or you weren't. It's likely that this thinking came from observing the natural world, in which we recognise leadership in a pack as being dependent on inherent traits; the biggest, strongest or loudest tend to lead while the smaller, weaker, quieter tend to follow. And while that might work in the Serengeti, the Daintree rainforest or the local woodland, we've come to learn that leadership is more nuanced in the human world of organisations and communities.

That said, it can be useful to analyse the apparent traits that successful leaders possess. While not being an exhaustive list, some of the more immediately recognisable domains are knowledge, emotional intelligence, confidence, honesty, energy, likeability, decision-making skills and flexibility.

The question here is, to what extent do you feel you can improve in each of these domains? If you adopt a mindset of 'you either have it or you don't', you're susceptible to what Professor Carol Dweck describes as a fixed mindset. We explore this in more detail in chapter 4, but broadly speaking if you hold a fixed mindset around your leadership you believe that if you're a natural leader there's no need to learn how to improve, while if you believe you aren't a natural leader, then you see no point trying to improve. You simply don't have what it takes. The good news is that there is also the growth mindset approach. As I mentioned, we dig into what mindset theories mean to you in chapter 4, but right now I'd like you to take a moment to consider the domains I listed above and what they mean to you.

And remember, there are no right or wrong answers.

Knowledge

How much do you know about your organisation, its processes, its people and its objectives? Is more knowledge always a good thing for you in your position? Do you know enough? How might you find out more about the things you really need to know?

....

....

....

....

Emotional intelligence

To what extent are you able to recognise and manage your emotions? Are you able to recognise and manage the emotions of others? To what extent can you read a room or do you sometimes miss the mark?

....

....

....

....

Confidence

How confident are you in your abilities? Does this confidence alter if you compare your confidence in your ability to get a job done versus your confidence in getting others to do a job? Are you confident in front of a group or do you have the confidence to handle tricky conversations in 1:1 meetings? How do you distinguish between confidence, ego and arrogance?

....

....

....

....

Honesty

How honest can you be with your people? Do they need to know everything? Is transparency always a good thing? Is there such a thing as being too honest? Do you ever find yourself needing to be 'brutally honest' with someone?

....

....

....

....

Energy

How much energy do you bring to your role? What kind of energy do you bring? Do you brighten or energise a room by walking in, or do you get the impression that maybe you brighten up the room by walking out?

....

....

....

....

Likeability

How important is it to you that your people like you? Do you ever find yourself holding back on an issue because of your desire to be liked? Alternatively, is your mantra, 'I'm not here to be liked. I'm here to do a job'?

....

....

....

....

Decision-making skills

Are you quick to make decisions or do you like to take your time? Do you need the input of as many people as possible or do you trust your own instincts? Do you have the confidence to pull the trigger, or do you tend to second-guess yourself and procrastinate?

....

....

....

....

Flexibility

Is it your way or the highway? Or do you tend to sway with the group? Do you hold fast on a decision or will you consistently review it? Do you give your people free range to go about their work however they wish or is there a strict process you ensure they adhere to?

....

....

....

....

Now let me guess your answer to each of those domains.

'It depends.'

And of course, it depends.

In fact, 'It depends' is usually my answer to any question I get in a workshop or Q&A panel. And while some people might feel this is a cop out, rather it recognises that life is complex and often issues have nuances that are context specific and temporal.

The important follow-up questions are, 'On what?' and then 'And how does that play out?'

Taking the hits for the team

I was consulting with Anya at a large manufacturing company. Over the previous 12 months she had been promoted internally to the position of National Head of Sales. She was now in charge of the people she used to work side by side with.

I'd been invited in because Anya hadn't made as productive a start in her new role as her boss would have liked. That's not to say she was doing a bad job — in fact, her team thought she was very supportive and an improvement on her predecessor. So what was going on?

We were having our initial chat over a cup of coffee at a café in the industrial park where the company was based. Leaving aside Anya's choice of coffee — decaf soy latte (not a coffee) — we got off to a good start. I heard about how Anya had been the first in her family to go to university and she seemed to be on a fast track to corporate success as her appointment to National Head of Sales had come relatively quickly. In fact, as we chatted I started to think that perhaps I was meeting with the wrong person. Anya was sharp, knew her stuff and seemed to be pretty well-read on leadership.

But then it happened.

Just as we were wrapping up and I was preparing to go back to the organisation to find out who I was supposed to be working with next, Anya received a text message. She let out a sigh and said, 'Sorry Dan, are we done? I have to get back. Something's come up and the team can't sort it out without me. It's the third time this year!'

It was February.

I tagged along as Anya went back to rescue the situation.

Evidently, a customer had a complaint and Anya was the only one they wanted to speak to.

On the surface not such an issue, but what transpired was quite interesting.

Over the past few months, Anya had taken to dealing with any complaints that came across the sales team's desk. She was great at diffusing situations and ensuring customer loyalty. The team loved this, of course, because it meant they didn't have to deal with the worst aspect of their job and saw Anya as taking the hits for the team. But it was now apparent. This is how to deal with complaints: pass them to Anya.

I realised that I had met with the right person and I started prepping for our next conversation.

You can probably already draw the lines between the various domains above and the predicament Anya found herself in.

If Anya was reflecting on the domains mentioned previously, her confidence and likeability reflection might sound like this:

Anya: 'Well, it depends.'

Me: 'On what?'

Anya: 'If we're hitting our numbers or not. If we need to keep this customer at all costs.'

Me: 'And how does that play out?'

Anya: 'Well, I'm confident handling tricky customers, but I'm not sure about others. It's just easier and safer to do it myself.'

Me: 'And how does that play out?'

Anya: 'In the short term pretty well — like, we keep the sale — but I know my team aren't developing and what's worse, they like me for it!'

Anya had found herself at what I call 'the leader's quandary', where leaders find themselves too busy doing other people's work, yet feel they can't address it for fear of losing the team. Over time, leaders find themselves exhausted and exasperated asking, 'Why can't they just do their jobs?'

The minute you notice your team aren't developing is the minute you realise you've stopped leading.

Are there any times you've been faced with the leader's quandary? Hint: these are the times when you've found yourself saying, 'Oh, don't worry, it'll only take me five minutes', 'Why don't they get it?' or 'It'll be quicker if I just do it myself'.

....

....

....

....

The key takeaway here is that these dispositions alone will not guarantee your success as a leader because leadership is about others, but they can serve as a conversation starter as you learn to adopt and adapt them to enhance your leadership.

'With great power comes great responsibility'

I'm not sure who said it first, but I do know that Uncle Ben said it to Peter Parker in the 2002 *Spider-Man* movie, and even though this is a popular social quote, it certainly holds.

It's impossible to lead without power or influence, but I'm assuming you haven't been bitten by a radioactive spider, so from where do you draw your power or influence?

One of the most well-known theories of power and influence is that of John French and Bertram Raven, in which they state that forms of power and influence are divided into two categories, positional and personal.

Let's deal with positional power first.

Positional power

Within this category, there are four types of power: legitimate, reward, coercive and informational.

Legitimate power

Legitimate power comes from being in a position of power in any organisation, such as the manager in a smaller organisation and the role of a CEO in a broader organisation. This type of power is dependent on the individual holding that position and on the hierarchies within organisations and communities. For example, should your manager lose their job, they no longer have the power to tell you when you can take leave; or while a prime minister might be able to introduce laws in their country, they are largely powerless to do the same in another. However, their position might allow them some influence.

Reward power

Reward power is primarily extended through setting rewards for individuals who are able to complete their set targets. Whether it's stickers for a child completing their homework or a multi-figure bonus for a CEO meeting their targets, this type of power is often used to encourage individuals to work harder with the promise of a reward if they do so. As we explore in chapter 8, an over-reliance on the extrinsic motivators required for reward power can actually serve to undermine productivity, team cohesion and your leadership in the long term.

Coercive power

If reward power has its drawbacks, then you need to be mindful of coercive power. The use (or abuse) of coercive power can include inducing a fear of losing employment, receiving a negative performance report, or the threat of being demoted and having perks taken away.

It's not uncommon for leaders and organisations to rely too heavily on coercive power, especially when trying to establish high-performance standards and expectations from employees. As we explore in chapter 6, these attempts are often misguided and while the need for consequences for poor performance is self-evident, an over-reliance on coercive power often creates lower standards, and, in the worst cases, a toxic work environment.

Informational power

You know that whole, 'I know a secret' feeling that you had when you were a kid? That's informational power. It's having control over information that others need or want and that puts you in a powerful position. You might know people who carry themselves differently when they know something you don't. They come out of a meeting, and they want you to know that they know something you don't. It's a classic power play that ultimately damages teams.

Today, in what is often referred to as the knowledge, or information, economy, having access to information is particularly powerful. But what's more powerful is what you do with it. Think of how many times terms like 'fake news' have been used over the past few years, or cases of insider trading have hit the headlines. Within your own organisation it might be smaller issues like who's up for the new position of regional manager, or who's going to keep or lose their jobs in the next round of budget cuts.

In its best form, informational power can be used to help and empower people. In its worst, it can be used as a weapon.

When it comes to power and influence, French and Raven suggest relying purely on positional power is fraught with challenges. You may well have had experience working with people who did just that. We don't want to be like them!

Personal power

The second category is personal power. French and Raven identify two types of personal power: expert and referent.

Expert power

Expert power stems from personal experiences, knowledge or skillset. With increasing experience across a particular field, we're able to become leaders in that space. Becoming a subject matter expert gives us a level of expert power because we're able to think a situation through and suggest solutions. You might know people who are the 'go-to' person in your organisation around various issues.

Referent power

This power comes from being revered. Rightly or wrongly, some people have the trust of many. This is one reason why you see many politicians clamouring for the support of celebrities. The public don't trust pollies, but they do trust their favourite musician, and if they say the politician's all right, then that's good enough for them. The challenge for leaders is not to rely on referent power overly, otherwise they end up in Anya's situation of not wanting to be disliked and that fear paralyses the leader from making the decisions they need to make.

###

The reality is, there's no secret solution to leadership. There's no one-size-fits-all approach. It's a continuous cycle of having an awareness of the scenario, deciding if something needs to be addressed and, if so, doing something that will address the situation and ideally create new awareness.

So with that in mind, when it comes to how you use your power, have you taken Uncle Ben's advice to heart? Do you use it responsibly? Where does your power as a leader come from? What do you need to be more aware of?

....

....

....

....

What's your style?

So far we've considered some theories. Now let's consider how this plays out in your actions. You've likely heard of Kurt Lewin's leadership styles framework—autocratic, democratic and laissez-faire—and while there are many other styles we could consider, this provides us with a good starting point in determining which elements of this book are going to be of most use for you.

The framework defined by Lewin presents different leadership styles with variations specifically around decision making and management.

Autocratic style

If you're an autocratic leader, you're keen to make your own decisions. In making these decisions, you're often detached from, and don't require any form of consultation with, your team. Sometimes these decisions are based on the personal opinion of the leader and are imposed across the organisation. This style of leadership is considered appropriate when there is no need for input, or if the skill gap between the leader and the team is too wide for them to make a meaningful contribution. This style allows for efficiency in some forms by removing the consultation process and streamlining the decision making to have a single point of contact.

Democratic style

A democratic leader involves the team and gives them a voice in the decision-making process. While the leader still holds the active role in the process, there's extensive involvement from other individuals in coming to a decision. This style is useful when the agreement of many people is central to the success of an initiative. Depending on the size of your organisation and a project's timeline, leaders might take a more or less favourable view of being democratic.

Laissez-faire style

A laissez-faire leader is deliberate in taking a 'hands-off' approach. They keep out of the way and allow the team to come to decisions themselves. For a laissez-faire approach to work, the team needs to be made up of highly capable team members who can problem-solve and have the authority to make decisions. A major stumbling block of this type of leadership is when leaders take a laissez-faire approach without giving the team the necessary authority to act as required. This leads to all manner of challenges, from laziness to lack of productivity and, in worse cases, a toxic workplace.

Can you identify when you lead in each of these styles?

I'm autocratic when:

....

....

....

....

I'm democratic when:

....

....

....

....

I'm laissez-faire when:

....

....

....

....

But I know what you're thinking. You're thinking, 'Dan, it all depends on the situation!'

And you're right, everything we've discussed in this chapter is dependent on the situation in which you and your team find yourself, and we explore in the next chapter how the impact of your situation can dramatically affect how you 'show up' as a leader, and how stress can affect your emotional and rational responses.

The Act of Leadership: Start with questions

For now, I urge you to reflect and consider, what does any of this mean for you? What do you tend towards with regard to your leadership style, or where and how do you derive your power? What traits do people see in you? Are they the traits you'd hope they see?

As you work through the book, you might keep coming back to your insights from this chapter.

On leadership traits

What leadership traits do I possess? What traits do I wish to develop?

....

....

....

....

Chapters 2, 3 and 5 are designed to help you get some insight into these questions.

The leader's quandary

Do I find myself in the leader's quandary more than I'd like? Who puts me there? What is the fallout for me and my team?

....

....

....

....

If you've found yourself in the leader's quandary more often than you'd like, then I've written chapters 8, 9, 11 and 12 especially for you.

Learn from Uncle Ben

How do I think about the power I have? How do I use that power to influence others? Am I always responsible with how I use my power?

....

....

....

....

If you're interested in how to use power or otherwise in your leadership, you might want to pay particular attention to chapters 6 and 9 and 10.

What's your style?

Do I like things done my own way? Do I try to please everyone? When am I 'hands on' or 'hands off'? Is that what my people need?

....

....

....

....

While not explicitly written to address each of the styles, you might find that most chapters will provide new insights if you tend towards being autocratic most of the time. Chapters 3, 4 and 7 may resonate.

For those times when you tend more towards being democratic or laissez-faire, chapters 11 and 12 will give you some specific insights about how to hold people to account and how to have what you might currently consider to be difficult conversations.

The sweet spot

After reading this chapter:

What new insight(s) do you have?

....

....

....

....

What new intention(s) do you have?

....

....

....

....

What action(s) will you start / stop / keep doing in order to enhance your leadership?

....

....

....

....

Chapter 2

BE MINDFUL, NOT MINDLESS

The importance of being in the moment

This chapter in a nutshell

- you'll explore the relationship between your Thinking Mind and your Feeling Mind

- you'll learn a technique to better regulate your response in stressful situations

- you'll be challenged to choose to show up as your best, both as a professional and in your personal life

One of my favourite pieces of research, and by extension favourite stories to share, explores the experiences of a group of seminarians back in the 1970s.

The Princeton Theological Seminary (PTS) sits within Princeton University, just south of New York, in the United States. Established in 1812, PTS defines itself as a school that unites piety of the heart with 'solid learning'. It is a training centre for church leaders that specialises in preaching—what they describe as 'the cure of souls', evangelism and missions.

People joining the priesthood tend to see it as a calling rather than just an avenue to fulltime employment. They internalise and embody the teachings of the Bible and use parables such as The Lost Coin, The Rich Fool and The Unmerciful Servant to preach and cure souls. Whether you know these three parables or not, I reckon you'd know the parable of The Good Samaritan.

It's a parable that Jesus shares in answer to a lawyer who asks how he can achieve eternal life.

Jesus responds, 'What is written in the law? How do you read it?'

The lawyer says, 'You shall love the Lord your God with all your heart, with all your soul, with all your strength, and with all your mind; and your neighbour as yourself'.

Jesus tells him, 'You have answered correctly. Do this, and you will live'.

But the lawyer, trying to get clear on what Jesus means, asks, 'Who is my neighbour?'

Rather than paraphrase, this is how it's told in Luke 10:30–37 of the *World English Bible*:

Jesus answered,

> A certain man was going down from Jerusalem to Jericho, and
> he fell among robbers, who both stripped him and beat him, and
> departed, leaving him half dead. By chance a certain priest was
> going down that way. When he saw him, he passed by on the
> other side. In the same way a Levite also, when he came to the
> place, and saw him, passed by on the other side. But a certain
> Samaritan, as he travelled, came where he was. When he saw
> him, he was moved with compassion, came to him, and bound
> up his wounds, pouring on oil and wine. He set him on his own
> animal, and brought him to an inn, and took care of him. On the
> next day, when he departed, he took out two denarii, gave them to
> the host, and said to him, 'Take care of him. Whatever you spend
> beyond that, I will repay you when I return.' Now which of these
> three do you think seemed to be a neighbour to him who fell
> among the robbers?

He said, 'He who showed mercy on him'.

Then Jesus said to him, 'Go and do likewise'.

So, let me ask you a question.

*What do you think would happen if a student from the PTS was walking
across campus and came across a stranger who was lying by the side
of the road, clearly in distress and in need of help? Note your prediction
and reasoning for it below:*

....

....

....

....

From Jerusalem to Jericho

About forty years ago, two Princeton social psychologists, John Darley and Dan Batson, asked each other the same question I just asked you.

But because Darley and Batson were social psychologists, rather than just guess they really wanted to know what does happen when a student from the PTS walks across campus and sees a stranger lying by the side of the road, clearly in distress and in need of help.

So in 1973 they set up an elaborate experiment with students from the PTS to find out.

Students were individually taken aside and told that in order for the teaching faculty to better understand how they were faring as they approached their forthcoming life in the priesthood, they would need to give a three- to five-minute talk.

They were either asked to speak about career and job opportunities outside of the ministry—in essence, in what other roles would having seminary experience be an asset? Or they were asked to read the Parable of the Good Samaritan—as you just did—and then craft their talk in response to it.

Students were told they wouldn't be allowed to use notes during the talk and so were given time to fully prepare. They were also told that their talk was going to be video recorded in an office in the next building, so that the faculty could review it later.

They were then shown a map with directions on where the talk was to be delivered, and were told to meet a secretary who would arrange for the talk to be recorded.

The students were then left alone to prepare their talk.

A short time later, as each student finalised their presentation, a member of the faculty returned to tell them one of three things:

- 'You're late. They were expecting you a few minutes ago ... You'd better hurry. It should only take a minute.' The researcher referred to this as the *high-hurry condition*.

- 'The (studio) assistant is ready for you, so please go right over.' This was the *intermediate-hurry condition*.

- 'It'll be a few minutes before they're ready for you, but you might as well head over. If you have to wait there, it shouldn't be long.' This was the *low-hurry condition*.

From Monday 14 to Wednesday 16 December 1970, Darley and Batson watched in the cold New Jersey winter as, one by one, students made their way across campus to deliver their talk, and what they observed was fascinating.

Students had to pass through a narrow alley to get to the next building, and in that alley was a man sitting slumped, head down with eyes closed, not moving. As each student passed through the alley, the man would cough twice and groan, keeping his head down, clearly in need of help. This man was in-fact an actor hired by the researchers.

How many of the students—who, just as a reminder, were studying to join the priesthood—would stop to help?

Probably not quite as many as you might think.

In fact, only 40 per cent of students offered any kind of aid, either directly stopping to attend to the 'victim' or mentioning it to another member of the faculty upon arriving at the office where the talk was to be given.

The vast majority of students who stopped to help were those who had been told, 'It'll be a few minutes before they're ready for you, but you might as well head on over. If you have to wait there, it shouldn't be long'. They weren't in a hurry.

Of those students who were told that they were late *only 10 per cent* stopped to render any kind of assistance.

Let's say that again. Only 10 per cent of students who had been told they were late stopped to offer assistance.

These students were studying to join the priesthood at a school that defines itself as a training centre for church leaders who specialise in 'the curing of souls', and half of whom were on campus with the sole purpose that day of discussing the importance of being a Good Samaritan, but when they were presented with the opportunity to be a Good Samaritan themselves, they chose to walk by, with the researchers noting:

> Indeed, on several occasions, a seminary student going to give his talk on the parable of the Good Samaritan literally stepped over the victim as he hurried on his way!

If you know of a better example of talking the talk, but not walking the walk, I'd love to hear it please.

It's not character but conditions

It might be easy to dismiss someone who steps over an injured person in the street as callous, but it transpires it has less to do with the character of an individual and more to do with the conditions in which they find themselves.

If someone is running late they are less likely to stop and render assistance.

When a person is in a hurry, something seems to happen that is akin to Tolman's (1948) concept of the 'narrowing of the cognitive map'. It turns out that it wasn't that the seminarians who were in a hurry didn't notice the victim—in the post-experiment interviews almost all mentioned him—or that they didn't think he might have been in need of help. Rather, it seems that in the moment they weren't able to work this out. Something blurred their perception of the scene.

The researchers concluded that rather than being callous and choosing to ignore an injured person, the seminarians fell foul of the impact of pressure and simply didn't perceive the scene in the alley as something that needed their attention.

For other seminarians, particularly those who were running late, Darley and Batson concluded that because the seminarians believed someone else was depending on him getting to a particular place quickly he was in a mental conflict between stopping to help the victim and continuing on to meet his commitment of recording his talk. And this is often true of people in a hurry; they hurry because somebody depends on their being somewhere. Conflict, rather than callousness, can explain their failure to stop.

It's safe to assume that most of these seminarians, if they had their time over would like to stop to render assistance. But I wonder, how often have you looked back on a situation and thought, 'What was I thinking?' or 'If I had my time over again I would definitely do things differently'.

Recall such a time. Note down how it played out, and upon reflection, if you had your time again, what you would do differently.

....

....

....

....

The two minds: Red and Blue

In his book *Emotional Intelligence: Why it can matter more than IQ*, Daniel Goleman states that 'In a very real sense we have two minds, one that thinks and one that feels'.

Broadly speaking, the Feeling Mind refers to the limbic system, the part of the brain involved in our behavioural and emotional responses. It is primarily occupied with ensuring our survival so it governs our feelings towards feeding, reproduction and caring for our young as well as our fight, flight or freeze responses. One of the most important components of the Feeling Mind is the amygdala, a collection of nuclei found deep within the temporal lobe.

The prefrontal cortex is — again broadly speaking — what Goleman is referring to when he describes the Thinking Mind.

The prefrontal cortex continually receives multiple sources of information and stimuli, processes these and adapts accordingly.

The Thinking Mind is responsible for:

- language

- managing and focusing our attention

- making predictions, particularly around the consequences of our actions or other aspects of our surrounds

- managing our emotional reaction and our impulse control

- our ability to plan for the future

- coordinating and adjusting our behaviours, particularly when step-by-step actions are required.

I will from here on, for reasons that will become clear later, refer to the Feeling Mind as 'Red', and the Thinking Mind as 'Blue'.

In order to navigate our day, Red and Blue work in harmony. Red is constantly on the lookout, keeping us safe, ensuring we understand the importance of each and every interaction, while Blue ensures we act accordingly with respect to our level of safety or importance.

Interestingly, in some cases the amygdala is thought to be able to process danger even before an individual is consciously aware of it. You might have experienced that yourself when you 'didn't have time to think'—you just acted—or when something 'just didn't feel right'.

Now while this is probably a positive, if, for example, you instinctively sway back from the roadside as a truck passes, or you reach out to hold your child back as they step towards a ledge, it's interesting to note that, while the amygdala is *quick to process threats*, it's not necessarily that adept at *distinguishing between threats*.

What I mean by that is, when it comes to physical threats, acting before you think might just save your life, but when it comes to what I call ego or identity threats, acting before you think might just cost you your job or a relationship.

Let's revisit the fight, flight or freeze response for a moment. This response is your body's natural reaction to danger. It's a type of stress response that helps you react to perceived threats such as an aggressive dog or noise in the middle of the night. It's all about self-preservation and it's likely an instinct that our long-lost ancestors relied on to survive. You see it borne out in nature documentaries when animals are preyed upon.

Some fight because they can. Perhaps they have a sting in their tail or venom in their fangs. Some run away (flight) because they back themselves to be quicker than what's chasing them. And some play dead (freeze), hoping that sooner or later the predator will leave them alone.

You'll have had similar responses if you've come across a snake in your garden, heard a noise in the dark, or felt a sense of unease in a crowd.

What's interesting to note is that you'll also have had similar reactions to ego threats or identity threats. Even when there's no possibility of physical harm, you'll have felt the urge to fight, fly or freeze, perhaps when you were asked a question in front of a large group, or when you received a curt email, or if you've found yourself in a verbal disagreement or argument in a staff meeting.

If you're prone to the fight response, Red mind would be telling you to arc up in the meeting, send a robust reply via email and cc all staff.

If you're prone to the flight response, the Red mind tells you to remove yourself from the situation, while if you're more likely to freeze, the Red mind tells you to cognitively 'play dead' and disengage from the situation.

Fortunately, however, the Blue mind is often on hand to help you navigate these situations. The Blue mind reminds you that blurting out exactly what you're thinking in the meeting might not be the wisest move, and perhaps a quiet side chat later on might be more beneficial in the long run. It's Blue that suggests to you that sending an email to all staff, including the CEO, at 1.23 am detailing just how wrong the new initiative is, might not be the best course of action in your career development, so Blue suggests you save it in your 'drafts' folder, safe in the knowledge you can revisit it tomorrow if you still feel the same.

It's Blue that detects that when someone who is a bit hot under the collar says to you, 'No, seriously, tell me exactly what you're thinking. I want to know', the smarter course of action is to temper your feedback.

And most of the time, Blue does a relatively good job of keeping Red in check.

But every now and then Blue doesn't get there in time. Every now and then we go Full Red. This can often happen after we've had a bad day, or a series of dramas. The words just come out and you lash out with real venom, maybe even physically.

Perhaps you do hit 'send' on that email and your sharp wit and incisive commentary lands in inboxes throughout the company, 'Ha! That'll show 'em', you think. Maybe you're so overcome by the flight response that you run out of the boardroom in tears or you freeze in the moment, like a deer in the headlights. If you're a parent, you've likely found yourself in situations with your children where, if you had your time again, you would handle it differently. You wouldn't fly off the handle, or say what you said.

How many of us have trodden on a piece of Lego after a hell of a day at work, and been like a volcano erupting, yelling as we throw the Lego that we bought (at considerable expense) in the bin.

After a short period of time, Blue comes back into the picture, and that's when you start Googling, 'How do I get emails back?'

As you're picking the Lego out of the bin, or sitting in the workplace bathroom drying your tears, you might find yourself asking, 'What was I thinking?' or hypothesising about what you would do if you could have your time again.

What would you do differently?

Do nothing — just breathe

Since you were young you've likely been advised to 'count to 10, or take a deep breath' in order to relax. It turns out that your parents' advice is based on some pretty sound reasoning.

In a state of relaxation, your body—and mind—is under the influence of the parasympathetic nervous system and as a result your breathing is slow and deep.

When you're experiencing the fight, flight or freeze response, you're being governed by the sympathetic nervous system and typically your breathing speeds up and becomes shallower.

However, what's interesting to note is that we can reverse the order of this relationship. We can choose to breathe slower and deeper to activate the parasympathetic system and calm down, relax and slow our heart rate. And it's in this state that we're far more likely to make mindful decisions that we won't regret later on.

Be more mindful. Don't bounce through the day mindlessly.

Being mindful of your breathing and being deliberate in slowing it down and inhaling deeper are skills that can be learned to help you make better decisions, handle disagreements more effectively, perform better in public speaking or, as was the case for Australian Rugby League player Chris Lawrence, save your life.

Having played more than 250 games in the Australian National Rugby League after making his professional debut as a 17-year-old representing Australia, Chris Lawrence is regarded as the consummate professional rugby league player. At the start of the 2019 season, as he and his Wests Tigers team were preparing for a game in New Zealand, Chris collided with one of his teammates and immediately knew he was in trouble.

He told me, 'Right away I knew I'd broken my jaw. I'd done it before and it kinda felt similar'.

All manner of thoughts rushed through his mind, from the disappointment of another injury to the thought that his contract was up at the end of the season and how this might affect the chances of an extension. This all happened before the instinctual reaction of reaching up to feel his face. That's when Chris knew he was in serious trouble.

'I could feel my face was caved in, and lying there, my teammates couldn't really look at me. Those who did catch my eye were visibly upset and shaken, and these are tough guys we're talking about.'

To make matters worse, there were no medical staff on the grounds other than the team physio, and it was clear that it was going to take a long time for the ambulance to arrive.

While waiting for the ambulance, Chris started to feel blood running down the back of his throat, and when the physio told him, 'We don't know when help's going to get here', he realised he needed to do something.

Actually, he needed to do nothing. He just needed to breathe.

Specifically, Chris focused on deliberately slowing his breathing down and as a result was able to regulate his stress response and lower his heart rate in order to remain calm and relaxed until help arrived.

When he finally received medical attention, it took days to diagnose the severity of his injuries. Surgeons likened it to what you might suffer in a car accident, and it was like nothing they'd seen in rugby league. As well as his jaw, he had broken every bone in his face. Even some of the broken bones had fractures in them. Countless metal plates had to be inserted into his face, but remarkably Lawrence was able to return to play before the end of the 2019 season, saying that the doctors and surgeons had reassured him his face was as strong as, if not stronger than, before the injury.

Chris Lawrence retired from the game in 2020 having played 253 first grade games and six games for Australia.

The Act of Leadership:
Choose to show up as your best

Don't worry, I'm not suggesting you need to suffer a major facial injury to get the benefit of this chapter, but I am going to encourage you to take a leaf out of Chris Lawrence's book about deliberate breathing and combine it with a technique that the New Zealand All Blacks Rugby Union team use that is called the Red/Blue Tool.

The Red/Blue Tool is the brainchild of forensic psychologist Dr Ceri Evans, who is regularly engaged by elite sporting teams, including the All Blacks, to help them perform under pressure.

In his book, *Perform Under Pressure*, Evans describes it as a three-step tool we can use to develop stronger emotional control. You'll remember how we previously described the Feeling Mind as Red, and the Thinking Mind as Blue. Evans's Red-Blue mind model requires you to consider a continuum with Red at one end and Blue at the other.

The three steps of the Red-Blue mind model are:

- *Step 1: Ask yourself, 'Red or Blue?'* Mentally locate yourself on the continuum. Just the act of asking yourself, 'Red or Blue?' brings Blue into the picture. Remember it's the Blue mind that's responsible for language. Whereas in the past we might have 'lost control', 'flown off the handle' or 'gone to pieces', asking ourselves a question stops us, and now we're faced with a choice: continue to let Red run the show, or move to step 2.

- *Step 2: Decide on a more effective response.* Quite often, a more effective response would be the course of action you'd take if you had your time again. Remember what you noted down earlier in the chapter? This is useful because more often than not, the situations in which we find ourselves experiencing the fight, flight or freeze response are similar, so there's real value in learning from previous experiences.

- *Step 3: Act in a more effective manner.* It's important to remember that Red doesn't mean bad, just as Blue doesn't mean good. Rather, Red motivates us to do something, while Blue ensures we do the right thing. We need a balance of Red and Blue. Nothing will send you Red quicker than trying to ignore your emotions!

Combining this with what we know about slow, deep breathing might result in a positive outcome, like Stefan's in the case study that follows.

Stop and take a deep breath

Stefan had had an awful day at the marketing agency where he worked. A project he'd been leading for months was suddenly – and in his mind, unfairly – scrapped by the client. The agency bosses were sympathetic to Stefan's point of view, but ultimately the decision was out of their hands, and Stefan would be tasked with driving another initiative.

As Stefan drove home, he played it over and over in his mind. All the hours he'd spent working on the project were wasted. The weekends he missed with his family as he strived to perfect the messaging of the campaign and the arguments he'd had with his partner about the hours he'd been putting in all now seemed to be for nothing.

He was in a foul mood, and the Sydney traffic wasn't helping. But as he drove, he remembered a workshop he'd attended in which the facilitator (me, as it turns out!) had suggested that a sh!t day at work doesn't need to mean a sh!t night at home. Stefan also recalled the Red-Blue mind model and the breathing activities we'd done.

When he got home, he sat outside his house for a few minutes and, with the engine and radio switched off, took a deep breath and asked himself, 'Red or Blue?'

He chose to walk into the house as the partner and parent he wanted to be. One that could be present and engaged with his kids and his partner. He said he even trod on a piece of Lego, and it wasn't that big a deal!

I know this because he emailed me the next day to tell me how a workshop that was designed to help him lead better had actually helped him partner and parent better.

Ask yourself, 'Red or Blue?'

- before walking into a meeting

- before picking up the phone to talk to *that* client

- before you walk in your front door at night (because a sh!t day at work doesn't need to mean a sh!t night at home)

- before you sit down to dinner

- before you talk to your kids about a drama they're having.

Jot down the situations that you know send you Red.

....

....

....

....

The more you practise being mindful, the more you'll find yourself able to regulate your emotional response. And the more you're able to do that, the better you'll lead, both at work and at home.

The sweet spot

After reading this chapter:

What new insight(s) do you have?

....

....

....

....

What new intention(s) do you have?

....

....

....

....

What action(s) will you start / stop / keep doing in order to enhance your leadership?

....

....

....

....

Chapter 3

ASSUME NOTHING

The biases that stop you from seeing what's really there

This chapter in a nutshell

- you'll be introduced to some of the most common cognitive biases that affect leadership

- you'll be asked to reflect on the biases that regularly show up for you

- you'll explore strategies to mitigate these biases

Okay, time for a little maths quiz.

What's 18 per cent of 50? And as they say at school, be sure to show your working out, and if you have more than one method be sure to show that too—and no, you can't use a calculator.

....

....

....

....

My preferred way of working out this, or any other percentage question, is to first of all flip it to see if it instantly becomes easier to my mind.

What I mean is: 18 per cent of 50 is the same as 50 per cent of 18, which to my mind at least is an easier calculation, especially without a calculator.

Now I only learned this in 2019, when freelance copywriter Ben Stephens tweeted this from his @stephens_ben account:

> Fascinating little life hack, for doing percentages: x% of y = y% of x. So, for example, if you needed to work out 4% of 75 in your head, just flip it and do 75% of 4, which is easier.

Stephens' tweet got retweeted more than 10000 times, liked more than 20000 times and was even reported on in the mainstream media by Sky News in the UK and News Corp in Australia.

However, it was interesting—as it always is—to scroll through the 600+ comments and replies to Stephens' tweet. It's not often you can put people easily into one of two categories, but in this case it was.

And, in relation to this maths concept, you will also likely fall into one of these categories.

The first category, and seemingly the majority, were the people who saw the tweet and had their 'minds blown'. It was revelatory to them, and something they couldn't quite believe was true. Interestingly, some of the people who fell into this camp also said publicly they were teachers, had applied degrees in mathematics or worked in STEM (Science, Technology, Engineering and Mathematics).

The second category of people were those who already knew this particular mathematic computation, and were staggered by, and dismissive of, the response of those for whom this was news.

Some responses bordered on vitriolic as they called into question the intellect of those who found the tweet a revelation. Some used it as an opportunity to attack the quality of the education system while others took aim at the news outlets who were reporting on the tweet.

There are few better places than Twitter to observe our human propensity to rip into strangers over minor issues based on assumptions and judgements. That said, there are many other places you can observe this too, including around your dinner table at home or boardroom at work.

Have you ever found yourself looking at someone who you know is smart, but they act as if they're not? Someone who you know has experience, qualifications and is paid to do the kind of work you're asking them to do, but for whatever reason, they just don't get it.

Wouldn't the workplace—and indeed, home life—be so much easier if everyone just saw the world the way you did? Wouldn't you be happier if people knew what you knew, believed what you believed and did what you wanted them to do?

As a kid, my mum used to tell me it would be a boring world if we were all the same, and while that's probably true, I meet a lot of leaders today who wish that people were the same. They wish their team had the same values, standards and behaviours as they did because it would make their life a lot easier.

It's also interesting to note that when leaders realise this isn't the case—that in fact, people are different with regard to what they see as being important or what constitutes professional behaviour—the default position many take is that their people are wrong.

This comes from two misguided beliefs:

- The way we perceive the world is the correct way.

- Others should perceive the world the way we do.

It's these two misguided beliefs that fuel most arguments on social media. As well as the maths question above, you might also recall a brouhaha about a blue or gold dress on Facebook some years back.

Most of the heated arguments you have around religion and politics, or arguments with your partner (or ex-partner), are perpetuated by these two shortcomings in our neural pathways and in many ways, this is the result of being human. The brain has to process so much information every second from multiple inputs that it simply has to put in short-cuts just so we can get through our day. If we were to consciously evaluate every snippet of data our brain received and processed it from every available perspective before determining from the myriad options available to us our choice with regard to words or actions, our most basic behaviours would be needlessly complex.

There's a considerable and continually growing library of research and insights around the workings of the brain, and it's not my intention to dig into that here. Rather, suffice to say, it seems we might not be as aware of the world around us, the decisions we make or the behaviours we exhibit as a leader as perhaps we think we are.

In short, we fall prey to our own cognitive biases. We make decisions believing we have the full, correct picture of things, when in actual fact we don't. We make assumptions about what other people think, say and do based on our world view, which we assume is correct when it is probably only 'correct' for us.

One way to tackle our cognitive biases is to simply be aware of them. Just by being conscious of the fact that the way you view the world is probably not true for everybody you work and live with, you can start to be a more mindful leader, partner or parent.

The literature around cognitive biases is mixed when it comes to just how many there are. Some authors suggest as few as 17, others suggest 25 or 53, while Wikipedia puts the number at well over 100. What I'm going to do here is take you through some of the common cognitive biases I see and hear and ask you to consider how they might play out for you.

Blindspot bias

> **You:** 'This is great; my team really need to read this; there are so many biases at play with them. It really annoys me.'
>
> **Me:** 'What about you? Do you think you struggle with any cognitive biases?'
>
> **You:** 'Nah, I'm fine with all this stuff.'

Here's the reality. You absolutely do have biases, but if one of those happens to be blindspot bias then you're unable to recognise it.

Whether you feel you might have a blindspot bias or not, I'd like you just as a thought exercise to work through the next few biases and see if anything strikes a chord. And yes, I'm aware of the irony, and that this is almost an effort in futility if you genuinely do have blindspot bias, but humour me, okay?

Curse of knowledge bias

If you suffer with the curse of knowledge, you assume that everyone knows what you know. You assume that they're all across a subject, the latest business process and the meaning behind the jargon you're using. One of the most common outcomes for leaders who suffer from the curse of knowledge is that work is not carried out as they expect. Money, time and resources get wasted because they assumed that work would be carried out in a particular fashion, but then in review they notice errors, or work that is not up to standard.

One of the simplest strategies to mitigate the curse of knowledge is to ascertain whether or not your team do understand.

However, try to avoid saying things like:

- *'Okay, is that straightforward?'* This implies it is relatively simple, and if they have any questions, perhaps they're not up to this.

- *'Does anyone have any questions?'* We explore in later chapters as to why this is not always the best question to ask, as more often than not, team members will keep quiet.

A better approach could be to say:

- *'Right, what questions do you have for me?'* This implies you expect and welcome questions.

We dig into the power of good questions throughout this book, as I firmly believe that by being armed with better questions, you can empower your team like never before, and avoid the pitfalls of many of these cognitive biases.

False consensus bias

You reach a false consensus when you believe that people agree with you more than they actually do. You might recall a time when it appeared that everyone agreed. You walked out of a meeting, or logged out of a Zoom call confident that everyone was on the same page only to find out down the track they weren't even in the same library!

Leaders beset by the false consensus bias misinterpret silence during discussions as tacit agreement and see the absence of disagreement as complete agreement. How many times have you thought to yourself, 'Why didn't they say anything in the meeting?'

The more often you find yourself saying this, the more likely it is that false consensus is a pet bias of yours.

As with the curse of knowledge bias, leaders can address false consensus with good questions asked in a culture in which dissent is welcome until a decision is made. In such environments, leaders are more concerned when team members don't speak up than when they do. In organisations that are mindful of false consensus, alarm bells ring if decisions are readily agreed upon too often.

Having a team and environment where people feel comfortable about sharing concerns and expressing disagreement is one of the best predictors of how effective that team will be. We explore more of this in chapter 6.

Confirmation bias

Have you ever sat watching an advert on TV in which a certain company is extolling the virtues of their product over another with statistics proving their case? Of course, you'll often then see a little asterisk somewhere detailing the research, or a disclaimer that suggests these results may not be typical.

What the companies have done is they've gone looking for and found the data that backs up their claim. They aren't making claims based on the data, they're finding the data based on the claims. But that's big companies right, looking to make a quick dollar. What's that got to do with us?

Well, it's quite likely that if you have a rocky relationship with someone—either professionally or personally—chances are you'll take the same approach as these wily advertisers. You go looking for, and find, the data that backs up your opinion of that person.

On a broader level, despite the world of science being against them, climate change sceptics can look for and find data that backs up their arguments, while smokers can find the one member of their family who 'smoked a pack a day and lived till they were 90!' to get well-meaning friends or partners off their case about giving up.

If you have a bad case of confirmation bias, you'll invest significant time and energy in proving your point, perhaps with scant evidence, rather than exploring the possibility of other perspectives.

To be an effective leader, you need to be wary of confirmation bias and be deliberate in seeking out and considering evidence that contradicts your own professional opinions.

If every piece of evidence you have to hand suggests you are correct, spend a little longer seeking out someone or something that offers a different perspective. This isn't designed to make you doubt yourself. In fact, the opposite is true: once you've sought out contradicting evidence and then worked together with your team—bearing in mind the blindspot bias, curse of knowledge bias and false consensus bias, of course—you'll be even more confident of your position.

Which leads us to …

Sunk cost fallacy bias

How often have you sat through a movie at the cinema that you weren't enjoying? This is a very low stakes example of the sunk cost fallacy. Because you've invested money and time in going to the movie, you feel compelled to see it out, even if it's not achieving what's generally considered the goal of going to the movies, which is to watch an enjoyable movie.

In the workplace you might see people refusing to let go of projects or clients because they've invested so much time in them already. Despite all the numbers and analysis showing that the project isn't working or the client isn't a good fit, still people persist. It's almost like they're a gambler down on their luck at the card table, but because they've lost so much money, they can't leave without trying to get at least some of it back.

But let's say that on the drive into work one day, you do realise that it's time to walk away from a project and try for something better — that's when you might be susceptible to one of my favourite biases.

Spotlight effect bias

Me: 'Why don't you go for that promotion?'

You: 'Oh I can't.'

Me: 'Why not?'

You: 'What would people think???'

Me: 'Nothing. They're all too busy worrying about what everyone thinks of them.'

The spotlight effect is where you think people are paying more attention to you than they are and can result in our being over-cautious about making decisions or mistakes for fear of being scrutinised or judged.

This can be over significant life choices, such as career choices or even relationship decisions, but it can also affect the smallest of micro-decisions: from what shirt to wear and what music to play in the office, to whether or not to have your camera on in a Zoom session for fear of what people might think about you.

I caught myself in 2020 rearranging my bookshelf in preparation for a Zoom call to ensure that the 'right' types of book were visible to others on the call. While I cringe when I think about it, I'll likely still do it should you and I ever have a chat over Zoom.

If you're limiting the choices you make, or, in the case of addressing the sunk cost fallacy above, find yourself unable to commit to a change of plan because of fear of what people might think, I urge you to reflect on this question:

If you didn't make that change, and you ended up getting fired because of it, what decision would your replacement make?

If you come to the conclusion that your replacement would likely start, stop or keep something, that might give you the nudge required to make the decision you know you need to make.

Fundamental attribution error bias

With all that said, once we've agreed that we want to welcome discussion that challenges ideas and that disagreement is welcome, we must be very wary of the fundamental attribution error bias.

This is a classic pitfall for us. With fundamental attribution error we judge others' actions based on their personality or behaviour, while we justify or excuse ours based on our circumstances.

Consider the following example.

You're in a meeting and Sami is obviously more focused on her phone than she is the meeting. In your mind this is because Sami isn't being as professional as she should be, and it's really starting to annoy you. When you mention it to her, she's vague and seems disinterested in your point of view about phones in meetings. This only serves to reinforce your opinion of her as less than professional.

A week later, your parent, who lives alone interstate, has had a fall at home and a neighbour has taken them to hospital. You're not sure how serious it is, and the neighbour has been keeping you updated via text messages through the morning. You're expecting the neighbour to update you any minute regarding some tests your parent has had. You haven't mentioned it to anyone as you like to keep these things private, but you're checking your phone every few minutes during the meeting, and you're aware that people have seen you. It's okay though because you know they'd surely understand if they knew what was going on.

Sami uses her phone in meetings because she is unprofessional. You use your phone in meetings because you have an issue to deal with.

The reality here is there's often a whole other story going on underneath the behaviour. In education, teachers are often taught a metaphor involving an iceberg to illustrate that the behaviour they see in their students is what's visible above the water; what lies beneath the surface are all the contributing factors. This is a direct effort to help teachers avoid fundamental attribution error.

In my experience, this bias is one of the biggest contributing factors to having 'difficult' conversations, something we look at in chapter 12.

Halo effect bias

The halo effect is where you observe an individual's positive character trait or competence in a specific domain and this causes you to overestimate their character or competence in other domains of their work or life. I contend that this is one of the reasons many leaders struggle when they first come into a leadership position, especially if they've been promoted from within the company.

There's more to leading than being good at your job

Consider Josh, a sales representative who consistently meets his targets, and is a well-liked member of the team. He's good at making sales, and he's a good guy!

Sometimes the halo effect might lead the organisation to assume Josh would make a great leader of the sales team.

As he assumes his new role, he's wary of asking for help (probably because of the spotlight effect) and over time a combination of these biases means that Josh doesn't develop as well as the organisation had hoped. He doesn't ask for help and the organisation isn't aware he needs it. As a result, the sales team performance begins to drop.

Sooner or later, a coach is brought in to help Josh, when really the original issue lies with the decision makers who were under the influence of the halo effect. The realisation that organisations need to make is that being good at sales doesn't necessarily make you a good leader of a sales team, even if you are a good guy!

Dunning-Kruger effect

As the saying goes, a little bit of knowledge is a dangerous thing. The Dunning–Kruger effect takes hold when people overestimate their abilities based on their limited experience or expertise. In short, their attitude outweighs their aptitude.

It's interesting to note that others can see this in you long before you see it yourself because, as it turns out, you don't have the necessary skills to realise you don't have the skills.

You can probably think of people in your organisation for whom this applies. That's easy.

The question is, when are there times that perhaps the Dunning–Kruger effect gets a hold of you?

In order to ensure that your team don't fall prey to any of these biases, I suggest you do all you can to mitigate the final bias we'll look at here.

Group-think bias

Me: 'Do you think you might have a case of false consensus bias here?'

You: 'No, no, no. We all really do get on and agree on everything. We never argue. We are incredibly harmonious. It's a great place to work.'

Me: 'Uh oh.'

Group think is different from false consensus because it occurs when people genuinely do want to agree. Sometimes this is to please the boss or to feel part of the in crowd, and in some cases it's because of a fear of rocking the boat.

It's like the peer group pressure of your teenage years, but rather than focusing on what hairstyle or music is cool, group think in an organisation can lead to irrational, costly, dangerous or even illegal behaviours—actually it's just like your teenage years!

There are all manner of high-profile cases where this bias has led to such outcomes. Whether it's the Australian cricket team using sandpaper on the ball, or banking institutions lending money to people they know can't afford it, you don't need to look far to see the impact of group think.

The questions are: Are you looking within your team and organisation? Where is group think leading you astray?

The Act of Leadership: Leave your assumptions at the door

You appreciate you're likely to succumb to cognitive biases from time to time, don't you?

Yes?

Excellent, you can skip the next three lines.

No?

Go back to the section on blindspot bias, work your way through, and I'll meet you back here shortly.

Once you've established that cognitive biases are at play—because you've realised that it's perfectly normal and human to have them, and your team is made up of humans—it's in your interest to be mindful of them. Here's what you can do.

Just having an awareness of these biases is the first step.

Your challenge is to be aware of them as often as possible. It might be helpful to have prompts on your laptop or office walls reminding you to consider the decisions you've made in the past week and evaluate your processes for making them. Did you lean on any of the biases more than you should have?

As well as looking back, you can get proactive.

Many organisations are well down the path of incorporating artificial intelligence, machine learning and algorithms into their decision-making processes. Removing the human propensity for bias means that if, based on the algorithm, a couple can't afford the mortgage, the bank simply refuses. The money isn't approved because the broker is taken out of the equation. There's no opportunity for the money to be loaned because a human succumbed to their biases and in turn fudged the numbers to make more profit for the bank.

However, my preferred mode of being proactive in avoiding bias is to have as diverse a team as possible.

Teams that are diverse with regard to gender, race, ethnicity, physical abilities, religious beliefs and other factors, are less susceptible to falling into these pitfalls than homogeneous groups and they tend to be more innovative. Add to that research from McKinsey that shows that public companies in the top quartile for ethnic and racial diversity in management were 35 per cent more likely to have financial returns above their industry mean, and that those in the top quartile for gender diversity were 15 per cent more likely to have returns above the industry mean.

In a 2016 *Harvard Business Review* article, David Rock and Heidi Grant went so far as to say that 'enriching your employee pool with representatives of different genders, races and nationalities is key for boosting your company's joint intellectual potential'. They maintain 'that creating a more diverse workplace will help to keep your team members' biases in check and make them question their assumptions'. Simultaneously, they say, organisations need to have inclusive practices that give everyone a voice. Rock and Grant believe that by adopting all of these strategies teams will be smarter and your organisation will be more successful.

If you're not in a position to influence the diversity in your organisation, at the very least I'd urge you to design your own Professional Learning Network (or PLN).

Despite this chapter starting off taking a sideways look at Twitter, I highly recommend it as a source of divergent thinkers, academics and practitioners.

You can curate your own list of people to follow, from your favourite leadership authors through to local, less well-known people who might be doing great things in your community.

Twitter has been my pseudo meeting room for many years because I deliberately seek out people whose views, backgrounds and expertise differ from my own, not so I can get into an argument with them, but so I can challenge my perspectives on issues to do with leadership, motivation and performance, and ultimately learn from them.

Head over to www.actofleadership.com for my Learning on Twitter guide.

And before you go: what's 80 per cent of 30?

The sweet spot

After reading this chapter:

What new insight(s) do you have?

....

....

....

....

What new intention(s) do you have?

....

....

....

....

What action(s) will you start / stop / keep doing in order to enhance your leadership?

....

....

....

....

Chapter 4

HOW TO TURN IT AROUND

Why you don't learn from your mistakes

This chapter in a nutshell

- you'll be introduced to Carol Dweck's mindset theory

- you'll be encouraged to reflect on how your mindset affects you professionally and personally

- you'll learn strategies to help you develop more of a growth mindset when required

Michael Jordan, the famed basketballer and arguably one of the world's greatest ever athletes, once said in a well-scripted Nike commercial, 'I've missed more than 9000 shots in my career. I've lost almost 300 games. Twenty-six times I've been trusted to take the game-winning shot and missed. I've failed over and over and over again in my life. And that is why I succeed'.

With quotes like this, and Insta memes aplenty, it's easy to get caught up in the romantic notion that we learn from our mistakes, that failure is our opportunity to improve and that a setback is just the beginning of our comeback.

But take a moment to recall the subject that you didn't do so well in at school. If you aced all your subjects in the senior years, there's a chance that you made choices in your junior years to let go of other subjects you didn't do so well in. Somewhere along the line you can think of a subject or class at school in which you didn't do well.

If you agree with Jordan's thinking, you should have succeeded in that subject, right? After all, you would have failed over and over and over again in that class? So why didn't you succeed?

Now while I actually do subscribe to Jordan's philosophy and believe it to be true, it's not true for everyone.

Perhaps even more specifically it's not for every mistake, failure or setback because it's not the mistake itself that causes the learning, but rather your response to the mistake. And your response is largely governed by two factors, one external and one internal.

The first factor is external, and it's the environment in which you make the mistake. This is influenced by the people around you, the culture of the organisation, and whether mistakes are acceptable and spoken about or swept under the rug and sought to be avoided at all costs.

The second factor is internal and one that you as an individual have more control over. Your mindset. Your mindset is your narrative. It's what you take into every single decision, every single interaction and every relationship. The reason you picked up this book in the first place, and the reason you're still reading it, is influenced by your mindset.

Think back to your school days. Was the reason you didn't learn from your mistakes because of the environment, or your mindset? Or was it a combination of the two?

We discuss the environment in more detail in chapter 6 where we explore how leaders can create a culture where it is 'safe' to make mistakes, but for now we'll focus on your mindset and how you approach your life and your relationships, your goals and the inevitable setbacks.

Carol Dweck PhD from Stanford University asserts that our mindset, whether fixed or growth, can determine our ability to develop new skills and improve existing ones.

Since Dweck's book *Mindset: The new psychology of success* was published, many in educational, sporting and corporate circles have started exploring the concepts of fixed and growth mindsets.

Fixed mindset

The fixed mindset originates from the entity theory of intellect, which people believe one is either born 'smart' or not. The fixed mindset doesn't only relate to intellect, it gets domain specific. Those who hold a fixed mindset believe that abilities, talents and characteristics are largely pre-determined, and if you don't have what it takes now, then it's unlikely you'll have it down the track. You'll often hear people express a fixed mindset about others when they say something like, 'Look, I'm not saying Ali's not smart, he's actually really clever. He's just not good with numbers', or 'Lisa's a great person, she's just not a natural leader. She just doesn't have what it takes'.

What we might not hear out loud as often are the stories we're telling ourselves about our own abilities, talents and characteristics. For example, I wonder what you tell yourself about the type of person you are, or what you're capable of. I wonder how many times you say, 'I'm not cut out for that', 'That's not my thing', 'I can't sing to save myself' or 'I don't have a creative bone in my body!' Or do you compare yourself to others and because 'they're a natural' and you're not, you place artificial limits on what it is you might be capable of? In fact, furthermore, you place artificial limits on even trying to find out what you're capable of.

We should be mindful, of course, that the fixed mindset doesn't only affect those who view their abilities, talents and characteristics as wanting, it also affects high performers. You might know of people who genuinely believe they are the smartest in the room, or they are simply natural leaders.

The point about the fixed mindset is, if I hold a deficit opinion of my abilities, talents and characteristics, there's no point trying. I don't have what it takes in the first place.

If, however, I believe myself to be an exceptional performer and I hold a fixed mindset about my abilities, then I shouldn't need to try. It just comes naturally.

Either of these two viewpoints can offer you an insight as to why people might not learn from their mistakes. Indeed, many people who hold a fixed mindset will do all they can to avoid making mistakes in the first place. The primary motivation for someone with a fixed mindset is to protect or prove themselves.

Some of the more common behaviours you'll observe when people are trying to protect or prove themselves follow.

Avoiding challenges

Would you rather be the best player on the worst team or the worst player on a better team? Even though, for a high performer, being the worst player on a better team is going to make you a better player, if you have a fixed mindset, you're not interested in that. You're not interested in getting better, you're interested in protecting your current status. A status that might be undermined if you challenged yourself and you weren't successful.

So, you avoid that challenge. You do just enough to prove to others that you could do it if you could be bothered.

You might have friends who seem incredibly competent but never go for that job promotion, citing all manner of reasons as to why it would be a silly decision to go for it.

You might have a team member who doesn't put their hand up in staff meetings around the boardroom table because they're scared that their idea won't pass muster.

Giving up easily

We can't avoid challenges forever. Sooner or later we're going to be presented with something that pushes us beyond what we think we're capable of. The inconvenient truth about a challenge is that it has to have a fair chance of failure. If it doesn't, then it's not really a challenge. It's just something else to add to your to-do list.

With a challenge, there's a chance you might not come up to the standards that either you or others set for you. And when you don't come up to those standards, if you have a fixed mindset, you give up. You say things like, 'That's it, we're done. I knew it wouldn't work. I told you it wasn't for me'. Or we seek to blame others: 'Pfft, those idiots on the interview panel wouldn't know a good candidate if they saw one! I knew they had it in for me from the start'. You'll often hear people talking about things 'not being fair' and feeling hard done by.

Effort equals incompetence

People with a fixed mindset do not see effort as the pathway to mastery, they see it as proof they aren't capable, or evidence of a system set against them.

Think back to your school days. How helpful was it when well-meaning parents and teachers implored you to just 'keep trying' or 'try harder'? Occasionally it might work, but for many the harder they tried the dumber they felt. Hard work and struggle become something to avoid.

At the other end of the ability spectrum, however, something really interesting is happening. Imagine the kid who, ever since they were nine or ten, has heard, 'Oh, she's brilliant, she's just a natural, we're so proud of her'.

There are three major problems with the pathway that parents have put their kids on when they speak like this. The first is obvious.

When adults say this about kids when they are so young, what they really mean is, they're the best little kid they know. They might be the top of their primary school class, they might be the best soccer player in their under 10s team or they might be the best violin player that the local music tutor has. They're a big fish in a little pond.

The second problem is less obvious.

The domain in which a 10-year-old demonstrates success is rarely a domain in which they have to work hard. What I mean by that is, the kid who is outperforming their peers in class, on the field or on the violin is in all likelihood not having to work that hard to shine. They've done all their hard work in the months and years prior. But then they get to 12 or 13 years of age and walk into a classroom or a change room or an orchestra pit with loads of other kids who were really good when they were 10. Now it turns out that while they didn't really have to try hard when they were 10 to be the best, all of a sudden they have to work their socks off just to be average.

And a lot of kids don't like that. They'd rather be that big fish in the little pond because effort is seen not as the pathway to mastery, but as proof that somehow they're losing their ability. You'll recall that in the fixed mindset, ability and success isn't just something they can do, it's who they are. In a fixed mindset, the need for effort can really challenge your sense of identity, which leads us to the third and even less obvious problem.

If Mum and Dad keep saying, 'Oh, we're so proud of you, you're wonderful at the piano. You're a wonderful mathematician. You're just a natural on the sports field', young people start to think that parents love them more when they're successful. The moment young people feel the affection of loved ones is tied to their success, they start wondering, 'Well, what does this mean for my parents? Do they still value me for this?'

Never has this been plainer for me than when I was working with an athlete who was the current under 18s champion in his sport. He looked me squarely in the eyes and said, 'My dad loves me more when I win'.

I appreciate we've taken a little detour from the normal route a leadership book might take, but it's critical to recognise that mindsets are formed in the early years, but carried throughout a lifetime.

Avoiding feedback (unless it's glowing)

Me: 'How well do you take feedback?'

Ninety-nine per cent of the people I ask: 'Depends who it's from.'

We take a deep dive into the world of feedback and conversations to help people improve in chapters 5, 11 and 12, but for now, suffice to say a lot of us ignore useful feedback.

If you've ever said, or heard, 'Seriously, how many times do I have to tell you?' then that's an indication of feedback that's gone, perhaps unheard, but definitely unacted upon.

Interestingly, if you're a high performer with a fixed mindset, you're more than happy to hear from anyone so long as the feedback is glowing, or fits with your world view. If you think you've done a good job, you'll say, 'I'd really welcome your feedback on that', whereas if you're less confident of your presentation, then that last line is missing from your talk or email.

Having sought feedback with the expectation of it being good, if it's anything other than that, you'll either dismiss the feedback giver based on the fact they don't understand your circumstances, or perhaps even question their character or their capacity to give you feedback. 'Who do they think they are?'

On the other hand, if you doubt your abilities, and your mindset is fixed, then rather than being a source of learning, any negative feedback serves to reinforce that the effort and challenge wasn't worth taking on in the first place. 'Seriously? What was I thinking, I'm not cut out for this!'

Resenting other people's success

In a fixed mindset, you can feel anxious about the success of others. You might feel a pang of jealousy, you might be suspicious or intimidated and you almost always resent it, and that can lead to interesting behaviours.

You may be able to connect the dots as to why high performers with fixed mindsets might feel compelled to cheat at the highest level in sport, or why corporate organisations and banks resort to unethical practices to stay ahead of their competitors. We need to recognise that these behaviours aren't merely a result of the pressure faced in the moment, whether an athlete is staring down the barrel of defeat or a CEO is looking at the third quarter in a row of reduced market share. Rather, I put it to you that this has been building for a long time, perhaps even for generations, and today we have individuals, teams and organisations who share a destructive narrative that says, 'Outward success is what we value you for; this is who you are. If you're successful, we love you. But if you aren't, well, it's not about a sport, it's not just a game. It's not just about profits or market share. This goes to the very fabric of who you are as a person and what you contribute to our relationship and the world'.

Growth mindset

Going back to Michael Jordan, we need to be prepared for failure.

It's around failure that growth mindset gets misinterpreted as the belief that you should never give up. But adopting a mindset of never giving up can be unhealthy. In fact you could argue that never giving up is more indicative of the fixed mindset because admitting defeat would be too big a blow to the ego, and what would people think of me?

Rather in a growth mindset we ensure that we don't give up *too soon*.

As Professor Carol Dweck told me during an interview for my podcast, 'We want people to know they can improve if they persist and not become derailed by setbacks that could be overcome. However, if they feel their efforts would be better placed elsewhere, that is also important'.

The Act of Leadership:
Lead with a growth mindset

As with most areas in psychology, the work of Carol Dweck hasn't gone unchallenged. Indeed many suggest that trying to educate people to have a growth mindset is futile. They might say that you either have it or you don't, without recognising the irony.

But it's important to recognise that a growth mindset is the belief that one's abilities, traits, behaviours and character can be developed through dedication and hard work.

That's it.

Growth mindset is not about telling penguins that they could fly if only they flapped their wings harder.

It's not about telling people they can achieve anything they want if they just believe hard enough.

It's the belief that, whether I'm the world's worst or the world's best, with hard work and effort I can learn, grow and develop. (Which is why Roger Federer still has a coach!)

And we can choose to adopt this belief.

And can choose to act differently.

We can choose to seek out and embrace a new challenge. It doesn't have to be anything huge. In fact, this book will suggest to you many micro-challenges that you could take on as a result of reading it.

It's not about good or bad

It's not a case that holding a fixed mindset is bad, or a growth mindset is good, and therefore should be pursued at all costs, because it turns out that it's not an either/or.

Professor Dweck told me, 'We are all a mixture of fixed and growth. We all have triggers that catapult us into fixed mindset thinking. It could be embarking on something difficult, struggling or receiving feedback. The key is to recognise when our fixed mindset is impacting our ability to improve at something we either want or need to improve at, and then to choose to adopt a more growth-orientated mindset'.

So, let's assume we hear our fixed mindset telling us to give up, but we choose to adopt our growth mindset and as such we determine that something is worth pursuing—then we need to view struggle as being valuable. In sport, many athletes talk about getting comfortable with being uncomfortable, and this approach is equally applicable for any endeavour, whether it be a new process at work or a new approach to parenting your teenager. You need to be okay with not being perfect, knowing that if you stick with it, you'll improve.

And when it comes to improving, there are few more powerful strategies than seeking useful feedback. You cannot be afraid of feedback that makes you think. We will explore feedback in-depth later in the book, but for now, think about who could help you think more deeply about how you show up.

Of course, it's likely you're going to have to find someone who is more capable than you. So instead of feeling threatened by those who are better than you, choose to find someone who inspires you. They are out there. You just need to find them.

Where are you directing your energy? Are you trying to prove yourself or improve yourself?

People who operate with a more fixed mindset tend to feel the need to protect or prove themselves and this could be on a daily basis, when faced with a particular situation or only when a specific person is in the room.

Those operating with a more growth mindset feel compelled to push or improve themselves and, regardless of the day, situation or people around them, they are interested in how they can learn, grow and develop.

If you direct your energy towards improving yourself, my best bet is you'll end up proving yourself without even trying.

Those who obsess about proving themselves, more often than not are encumbered by the behaviours brought about by the fixed mindset.

I often ask my clients to reflect on the following questions before walking into a board meeting or, in the case of athletes, a video feedback session:

- Am I trying to prove myself or improve myself?

- Am I trying to protect what I have or push myself to learn, grow and develop?

- Is this helping or harming me or those around me?

I've even had clients tell me they've started asking themselves these questions at home.

Now that you've read chapters 2 and 3, you'll be aware that maybe you shouldn't believe everything you think, particularly if you're a bit Red. And we're always a bit Red when faced with a failure or setback!

So, let's talk about you.

What's an area of your life in which you'd love to, or you know you need to, learn, grow or develop? This can be professional or personal. Write it here.

In the next six months, I would love to (or I need to) learn, grow or develop ...

....

....

....

....

Up until this point, what would constitute a challenge for you in this regard? What can you actively seek to do in the next six months to help you learn, grow or develop? Remember, there has to be a sense that you might not achieve it in its entirety for it to constitute a real challenge.

Detail some of the steps you will have to take in order to tackle this challenge.

....

....

....

....

Automatic negative thoughts (ANTs)

Now let's deal with setbacks, so we can be a little more like Michael Jordan when the going gets tough.

When we suffer a setback, we almost always experience automatic negative thoughts, or ANTs.

ANTs are perfectly normal—by definition, they happen by virtue of being human—automatically. In fact, if you experience a 'setback' and don't have negative thoughts, then it wasn't really a setback (or you're a sociopath incapable of experiencing negative emotions!).

By now you'll know that ANTs are largely the work of the Red mind, but by using our techniques to stop and reflect we're now able to be more mindful of these, and see which show up for us.

Catastrophising

Catastrophising is the tendency to overstate the significance of a setback—for example, 'It's a disaster!' or 'Things will never be the same again!'

When do you catastrophise?

....

....

....

....

Black and white thinking

This is the tendency to think it's a case of all or nothing—for example, when people ask us, 'Is it really that bad?' We respond with, '*Of course it is!*'

When do you think in black and white?

....

....

....

....

Personalising

Personalising is the tendency to see the reason for the setback as being solely due to who we (or others) are as people—for example, 'I'm a loser', 'I'm an idiot', 'It's all your fault' or 'She's clueless!'

When do you personalise?

....

....

....

....

Mindreading

This is the tendency to believe we know what people are really thinking—for example, 'They can't stand me' or 'He thinks I don't know what I'm doing!'

When do you mindread?

....

....

....

....

Over-generalising

Over-generalising is the tendency to believe these things 'always' happen to us, or we 'never' get listened to or that 'everyone' thinks we're an idiot.

When do you over-generalise?

....

....

....

....

Filtering

Filtering is the tendency to obsess on the negatives at the expense of the positives—for example, writing off a whole initiative as a failure because some aspects didn't work as well as we might have hoped.

When do you filter?

....

....

....

....

Taking time to recognise which ANTs show up for us is critical if we're going to challenge our mindset when faced with setbacks.

If you can name them, then you can tame them.

By listening out for the language we're using to describe ourselves, another person or a situation, we're better placed to challenge whether that narrative is true or whether it's just the Red mind messing with us.

If you take on a new challenge, there will be setbacks. It's not the setback that matters, but how you react. And that's going to take effort.

Sometimes we require extra effort not only to do more or try new things, but to stop doing something or to let something go. Below (see figure 4.1) is an activity I started doing with elite athletes before realising that it could work for people regardless of their professional or personal context.

It's called 'bridging the gap' and it looks like this.

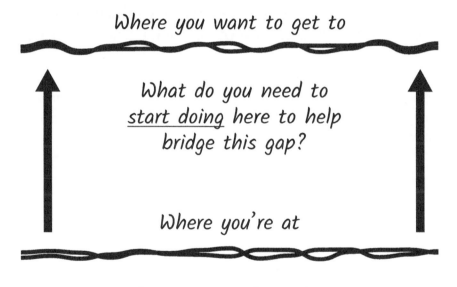

Where you want to get to

What do you need to start doing here to help bridge this gap?

Where you're at

What are you doing here which you need to stop or let go of in order to bridge the gap?

Figure 4.1: bridging the gap

Once you've established the things you need to do more of, and the things you need to let go of, tell someone. Or tell a group of people you trust. The reason for doing this is that you're going to enlist these people to give you feedback along the way.

You can choose to have people offer you ideas on how to achieve your new behaviours, but I'd also encourage you to enlist some people who simply check in with you and ask you questions about what you're doing. They don't need to be experts in the field, but rather people you trust and can chat openly with about what you're doing without any fear of judgement.

At this stage of the process, of course, we're interested in the results you're getting, but we're not overly focused on them.

We want to move away from a mindset of judgement towards one of curiosity and learning.

Who could you enlist in your tribe and what would you ask them for? Remember they don't necessarily need to be experts, colleagues or family. You could tap into your newly created professional learning network as discussed in chapter 3.

....

....

....

....

....

....

....

While your tribe needs to be available to you on some level to give you feedback, when it comes to looking towards successful people, start with whoever you regard to be the best at whatever it is you're trying to learn, grow or develop in.

Note down who they are and what it is about them that inspires you. Prior to this, you might have resented their success or been jealous about it. You might have seen their status as unjustly or unfairly gained, but now, having considered your position, you realise that you could learn something from them. In his book, *The Infinite Game*, Simon Sinek discusses the concept of having a 'Worthy Rival', someone who is worthy of comparison so that if we choose to study them, they can reveal to us our own opportunities for improvement. I'd suggest that high performers *need* others around them who can push them physically and mentally in order for them to truly see what they are capable of.

For example, I wonder, would Roger Federer be happier had Rafael Nadal and Novak Djokovic not picked up a tennis racquet when they were young? Or did Roger Federer only become the tennis player he became because of Nadal or Djokovic?

When I spoke to four-time Olympian Anna Meares about this idea, she spoke of her arch-rival, British cyclist Victoria Pendleton.

For years they had gone wheel to wheel in velodromes around the world, and things had become somewhat tense between the pair. One strategy to approach this rivalry would be for Anna to go away and learn all about Pendleton and her weaknesses so she could then exploit them to her advantage.

But instead, her coach introduced her to *The Art of the Samurai*, which extolls the virtue of studying one's rivals (or knowing thy enemy) not only to learn about them, but more importantly to learn about oneself.

She told me, 'This project lasted about three to four years. Many people thought this was about me getting to know Victoria Pendleton.

But it was really about me getting to know *me* through learning about my opponent. We reduced her performances to statistical data to remove the emotion from the rivalry, and by understanding Victoria's strengths and weaknesses, I was able to upskill myself. I had to break down old habits and learn new skills'.

Anna Meares is the only Australian to win individual medals at four consecutive Olympic Games and is regarded as the best female track cyclist of all time. She credits having a worthy rival as one of the reasons she was able to achieve this, saying, 'If it wasn't for Victoria Pendleton I wouldn't have had the desire to push myself in order to get better'.

Who can you learn about in order to learn more about yourself? Who inspires you? Who is your worthy rival?

....

....

....

....

The sweet spot

After reading this chapter:

What new insight(s) do you have?

....

....

....

What new intention(s) do you have?

....

....

....

What action(s) will you start / stop / keep doing in order to enhance your leadership?

....

....

....

....

Part II

THE 'YOU AND THEM' STUFF

Part II focuses on creating and nurturing the environments in which you and your team do your best work.

Chapter 5

MUM
WAS WRONG

It really *does* matter
what others think of you

This chapter in a nutshell

- you'll see why Mum was wrong, and why it does matter what others think of you

- you'll see why traditional efforts at 360 feedback sometimes miss the mark

- you'll be shown a 360 feedback technique that is far more likely to help you learn, grow and develop as a leader

The purpose of coaching is to help people to learn, grow and develop. In essence, it's to nurture a growth mindset in the people I'm working with.

The coaching process I use is based on the frameworks shown in figures 5.1 and 5.2.

The development of a leader—or any role for that matter—can be thought of as a triangle, as illustrated in figure 5.1.

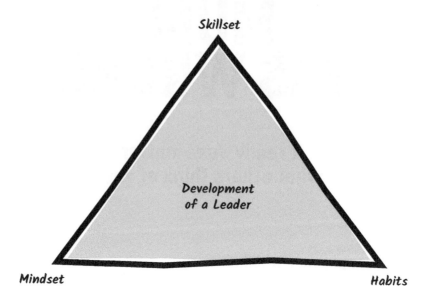

Figure 5.1: development of a leader

When we think of development, we often think of gaining more knowledge or skills, but maybe we don't spend enough time exploring the mindset and habits required to develop. That's where coaching comes in.

Remember, my coaching lens looks like this:

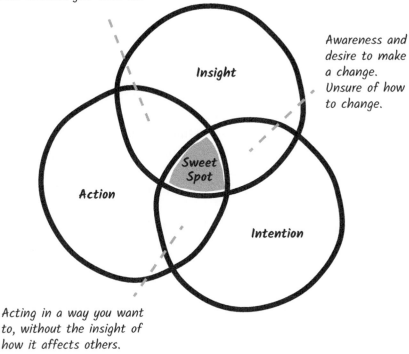

Acting in a manner based on insights
about others. However, you do this
because you feel compelled to rather
than because you want to.

Insight

Awareness and
desire to make
a change.
Unsure of how
to change.

Sweet
Spot

Action

Intention

Acting in a way you want
to, without the insight of
how it affects others.

Figure 5.2: the sweet spot of coaching

The sweet spot of coaching is where we use insights to motivate ourselves to act in a new way that—as well as improving performance—provides us with new insights.

As explored in part I of this book, we sometimes lack awareness of how we 'show up' in the world. The 360 feedback approach was designed in part to help leaders have more awareness about how their behaviours affect others.

However, as these surveys have taken on more importance with regard to performance reviews, promotions, HR and so on, they have begun to lose their effectiveness.

Rather than using them to improve, many people go into these processes looking to *prove* a point. I've had my own experience of organisations trying to prove that their people aren't the right fit for a role, or leaders looking for the feedback that proves they are performing well in their role.

I know that the first few times I used a 360 feedback tool with leaders, it was pretty much a waste of time. They'd skim read the feedback document, share a little knowing smile here and there, maybe a nod. There was always a sigh and a shake of the head at some point. Invariably there would be a stifled laugh and then they would conclude with another nod, while doing that expression people do when they turn down the corners of their mouths — like the opposite of a smile — that kind of says, 'Interesting, but not correct'.

They'd then gently toss the paper back on the desk, lean back in their chair and opt for a variation on one of these three responses:

- 'Yep, that's about right.'

- 'Wow, they didn't hold back!'

- 'I've heard it all before.'

Then, as I attempted to dig deeper, the coachee would do all they could to stay on the surface by focusing on the feedback they agreed with or that painted them in a good light. When I shifted their attention to elements of the feedback that were perhaps less than favourable, they would look to deflect, deny, blame or make excuses for it. This was true even if the feedback was neutral.

They would say things like, 'Yeah, but that's only their opinion', or 'They don't understand the nature of my role' in order to navigate the conversation, and more times than I can remember I heard a variation of, 'Yeah, but I don't worry about what people think of me. I just do my job'. This meant it was difficult to help the coachee create tangible actions to improve. So they didn't.

How often have you heard that, or perhaps even advised others to not worry about what people think?

I know as parents, my wife and I counsel my kids to pay no mind to comments in the playground, and, as they enter their teenage years, no doubt this will extend to interactions on social media and the like. Indeed, in my work with elite athletes they have to deal with 'feedback' from thousands of people online after a poor on-field performance, and our most common strategy is, 'Don't read it'.

In these two scenarios, the strategy of ignoring what others are saying about you is a good one.

However, sometimes this well-intentioned start-point can morph into, 'It doesn't matter what *anyone* thinks of me'.

And while this might sound like an empowering mindset to adopt, invariably it is problematic.

A better position to hold might be:

'It doesn't matter what *every*one thinks of me'.

In the case of a professional footballer, of course it doesn't matter what everyone thinks of them. But whose opinion does matter? The more experienced players I work with typically have a trusted network of people they listen to, usually their coach, their teammates and their family. No-one else's opinion on their performance matters.

As a leader, whose opinion matters most to you?

Your answer to this question will largely determine how effective a 360 feedback survey will prove for you. It will also determine whether or not you do anything to improve as a result of receiving 360 feedback.

But your answer will also be determined by the lead-up to, the quality of and the follow-up on the 360 feedback, and, in my experience, too many organisations get one or more of these areas wrong, and as a result limit the impact of their efforts.

What we get wrong with 360 feedback

Despite 360 feedback being a mainstay of the corporate world, there are several common missteps organisations make that ultimately dilute its effectiveness at helping people to improve. Let's have a look at some of them.

It's an event

When feedback is seen as an event, rather than just something we do regularly, it can take on more importance and the stakes are higher. Remember, 360 feedback should be about learning. Learning rarely takes place when it's high stakes.

There's no discussion

I've seen countless instances where there has been little or no discussion with the leader, their line managers, peers or direct reports about the rationale behind taking part in the 360. While we might assume that people understand the how and why of the process, as I hope has become abundantly clear by now, we should never assume! If people lack the clarity on why something is happening, they will invariably make up their own narrative. 'Oh, she's under-performing', or 'Am I next?'

The subject of the feedback wasn't in on it

The worst-case scenario is when the person is not part of the decision to use a 360 tool. This is often the case with middle managers, who have the process foisted upon them. They don't have an understanding of where this is coming from, or where it's going and may have thoughts such as, 'Will this affect my career pathway? Has someone made a complaint? Am I underperforming? Why isn't anyone else doing this?'

The quality of feedback

Many 360 feedback surveys work the same way, distilling the various competencies of leaders into types of behaviour, and then asking line managers, peers and direct reports to assess an individual based on those behaviours.

This can pose a problem when the questions elicit the wrong kind of data.

For example, if a survey item asks you to 'Rate Dan's ability to give constructive and helpful feedback', you'll likely rate my ability to give helpful feedback relative to your own. That is, if you think I'm better than you at giving feedback, you'll likely rate me higher, but if you feel you are more adept at giving feedback, then you'll score me lower.

Consider how you might rate someone you work with in these areas:

- their ability to handle conflict in an appropriate manner

- whether they are a problem solver

- whether they keep control of their emotions and behaviour even when involved in high-pressure situations.

There's no objective measure of these items. Rather, your frame of reference usually becomes your ability, or that of others in your immediate circle, rather than that of the subject of the 360. This is compounded when surveys ask you to rate individuals about their general behaviours across an organisation. In many cases you're just guessing. For example, you have no idea how constructive or helpful my feedback is to other members of the organisation.

Rating a person's ability in managing conflict by comparing it to our own is flawed, and yet that type of data usually makes up the majority of feedback in 360s. This is why many people will feel compelled to brush it off, argue against it or ignore it altogether.

And this is the issue. As we've already explored in part I of this book, you have many biases, most that you are unaware of, that skew the way you view the world and the people in it. Add into the mix variables such as age, experience or race and you start to get a glimpse of just how unreliable this data might be. And it's unlikely that the rest of the survey respondents will even this out. They're just as unreliable as you, and the sample size is too small to account for this. There's a reason polling companies ask thousands of people their opinion on something before it's taken seriously, and even then they sometimes get it wrong. We've seen this recently in the US, Australian and EU elections, for example.

However, if we ask these questions in a more nuanced way we can elicit better data. For example:

'Rate Dan's ability to give constructive and helpful feedback'

becomes:

'In your interactions with Dan, how helpful and constructive has his feedback proven for you?'

Now we can look for trends that actually mean something. If 70 per cent of my responders rate me low on this question, then this provides me with a useful insight that's reliable.

But once we get this insight, we hit the biggest issue of all.

No accountability for follow-up

I had something of an epiphany when I was sitting with Pierre. Originally from France, Pierre was now marketing director at a large, publicly listed company based in Sydney. I'd known him for a year or so courtesy of facilitating some in-house training on emotional intelligence and mindset for leaders. He'd completed a 360 feedback survey and the general manager had asked me to debrief him on the feedback and chart some next steps.

'So what do you think?' I asked.

He sat back in his chair, tossed the paper onto the table and said, 'Yep, that's about right'.

'Really? What specifically is right about it?' I asked.

'I need to delegate better,' he said. 'That's something I've heard a lot before.'

'So why are we still hearing it mate?'

I discovered that Pierre had attempted to improve his delegation skills by working with a coach and according to the coach, and Pierre himself, he had become better at delegating.

However, the most important people in the delegation process — his direct reports — hadn't been brought along for the ride. The coaching was somewhat secret; in fact, most of Pierre's team had no idea he even had a coach. Over time, the need to develop his delegation skills slipped off his radar and no-one was any the wiser it was ever even on it.

Ask yourself, who is best placed to give you advice on how to delegate?

In fact, circle back to the question I asked you early in this chapter: Whose opinion matters most to you when it comes to how well you delegate?

It seems to me that if you don't bring your team—the people you delegate to—along for the ride, you're not only limiting the impact of your 360 feedback, but you're also reducing the return on investment (ROI) on any subsequent coaching.

Leadership is about other people. Bring them with you. Let me show you how.

The Act of Leadership:
Ask for 360 feedback as a habit

As an executive coach there are many accreditations one can get. One that I have found very powerful in informing my approach to 360 feedback and the subsequent development of leaders is Marshall Goldsmith's Stakeholder Centered Coaching®.

Goldsmith is the author of many books, my favourite being *What Got You Here Won't Get You There*. It's one you might like to read after this one!

I became accredited in this way of coaching in the past few years, but had developed a similar approach in my own work. What follows is an amalgamation of the two, and is situated squarely on the foundation that the people best positioned to assess whether or not a leader has enhanced their skills are the people they lead.

I've come to realise that, early on, I was complicit in creating an environment that wasn't conducive to leader development. I looked at what were the accepted norms around such a process and went with it. However, over the past few years, I've taken a vastly different approach, and I encourage you to consider this, or a similar approach, for yourself.

Think back to our triangle of leader development (see figure 5.1): 360 feedback should not be an event, it should be a habit, and you should enter into it with the right mindset.

In fact, it should be a habit for everyone in the organisation, and it should be focused on learning, growth and development, and not tied to performance management.

I'm not suggesting that you should be completing 360 feedback surveys every month, but rather that having a time to check in regularly with colleagues to receive and share some feedback can be very powerful.

This approach can be as formal or as informal as you like. For the moment, we'll assume that you, as a leader, would like to embark on this journey to develop your own leadership skills.

The set-up

Despite this being about you, your direct reports will think it's about them. They might feel that, if identified, their responses could be held against them. Or that this is the thin end of the wedge, and soon everyone will be doing this as part of their performance reviews. Yes, you've guessed it, Red mind is in the driver's seat, and that could present you with some issues.

As the leader, you need to do your best work to alleviate any such concerns. One way you might go about this is to bring it up in a meeting, or via an email.

> Dear All,
>
> I've just finished reading a book that has really made me think about how I go about developing as a leader. I'm interested in exploring ways to create a culture of learning, growth and development here and I feel that I might be able to role model that through this approach.
>
> In two weeks I'll email you a link to complete an anonymous survey about my leadership, specifically as it relates to you.
>
> I'll then process this feedback [with my coach (delete if n/a)] and share with you my learning goals for the next six to nine months.
>
> I'm undertaking this as part of my own professional learning, and it is not tied to any organisational or HR processes. Please rest assured that no-one will ask you to take part in this process should you not wish to.
>
> If you have any questions, please let me know.
>
> I'm really looking forward to seeing where this goes.
>
> Kind regards,

The survey

When it's time to send the survey, you might use an external provider. Just please be sure to talk to them about the reliability of the questions as we discussed earlier in the chapter. You could also grab a template from www.actofleadership.com or you might choose to develop your own questions and set up your own survey form through Google, Survey Monkey or the like.

Remember, it's important that respondents know that while their responses are anonymous, open-ended answers will be fed back to you verbatim.

When you send the survey out, try to send it to as many people as possible. Ensure that you have a mix of peers and line managers, if possible, as well as direct reports.

Assuming that you are administering the 360 feedback survey yourself, you want to give at least one to two weeks for people to fill in the survey, sending reminder emails at least twice during that time frame. Of course, you will need to send reminders to everyone because you won't be able to discern who is yet to complete the survey. If you were to engage a coaching company to administer the 360, then they would handle all of this.

During this time, you will also complete a survey that addresses the same issues you're asking your people about. For example, if I'm asking my people, 'In your interactions with Dan, how helpful and constructive has his feedback proven for you?', I'm asking myself, 'Do I provide helpful and constructive feedback to my team?'

We can then compare our own reflections with those of our people.

Feedback stage

Prior to receiving your feedback, you might want to practise some of the breathing we spoke about in chapter 2. You might want to consciously choose to engage your Blue mind in order to avoid the most common pitfalls I see when people receive their 360 feedback.

It's not uncommon to see people experience shock, anger, defensiveness or denial before they resort to the three common responses I mentioned at the start of the chapter:

- 'Yep, that's about right.'

- 'Wow, they didn't hold back!'

- 'I've heard it all before.'

Another thing people try to do, either in their head, or out loud, is to guess who said what. Despite my imploring them not to even try, they do. And of course, when faced with similar scenarios, I too attempt to figure out who has said what about me.

For many of us, receiving feedback is hard because it typically sets off one of three tripwires in our thinking, and these tripwires are all connected to Red mind.

- Tripwire #1—We don't believe it: 'They're wrong!'

- Tripwire #2—It depends who it's from: 'Who are they to tell me that?'

- Tripwire #3—It's personal: 'Maybe they're right. Maybe I'm an impostor.'

These tripwires are all perfectly normal and to be expected, but at some point, if the 360 feedback process is to be useful, we need to choose to reset those tripwires and get Blue mind back in control.

When you compare your assessment of yourself against the feedback from your people:

- What do you notice you agree on?

- What do you notice might be some blind spots (i.e. their responses don't match up with yours)?

- What do you find interesting about the relationship between what you've said and what your people have said?

- What would you like to find out more about?

- What behaviour(s) or skill(s) strike you as being important to learn, grow and develop?

It's the answers to the last question that provide you with your learning goals.

Bringing your people with you

Once you've processed the feedback, the first thing to do is send an email to all the people you invited to submit feedback. Your only obligation here is to thank them. Again you don't know if they completed it or not due to the anonymous nature of the survey, but it's important to publicly express your gratitude.

Now it's time to build a learning team around you who can help you develop as a leader. Remember Pierre. He needed to delegate better. If this was your learning goal, who would be the people best placed to help you do that?

You want to assemble a team of about five to eight people who are going to help you develop. Who you choose will depend on the learning goal you've set.

If your learning goal is around how you interact with your direct reports, then the majority of your team should be direct reports. However, if your learning goal is more orientated towards how you interact with clients, then consider how you might engage them in the process. If you're interested in developing how you operate across functions, ensuring that you have representation from different departments is important.

Regardless of who you choose to join your learning team, it's important that they meet these three criteria:

1. They aren't your cheerleaders.

2. They aren't your fiercest critics.

3. They are willing to grow with you.

Once you've identified who these people are, in a meeting or via email, you invite them to join you in the learning team.

You might say something like this:

Dear [INSERT NAME]

As you know, I have just completed a 360 leadership survey designed to provide feedback on my leadership. It was a very insightful process and provides an opportunity for me to improve as a leader.

It was interesting to see what people thought about my leadership, and where they thought I demonstrated skill. For example, it's important for me to adapt and respond to change well (especially during 2020!) so it was gratifying to see that reflected back to me as something I do well.

The report also provided me with useful information on some leadership areas in which I want to grow.

Based on this feedback I have decided to focus my leadership growth in the coming year on:

- How I provide effective coaching for my direct reports

- How I can delegate more effectively

- How I can provide more effective feedback.

So now I would like to invite you to continue to support me in my process of growth and change. I'm putting together a learning team to help me stay focused on my learning goals. I'm inviting you to be part of this process because I value your constructive input and I know you will be honest and fair.

I shall ensure that being a part of the team will not be a burden on your time.

Could you please reply as to whether you would like to be part of the process moving forward.

Kind regards,

Once you've assembled your team, the process is simple.

Focus on one or more of your learning goals, and ask your team for one or two suggestions as to how you might improve in this regard. This can be done face to face as part of your regular 1:1 meetings, or via email:

What are one or two things I could do (or stop doing) that would help me provide more effective coaching for my direct reports?

Assuming you have eight people in your team, and all eight provide two suggestions, you'll end up with 16 ideas. Choose one or two.

Then share back to the team what you are focusing on, and give them a time frame, ideally 30 days:

Thank you for all your suggestions. For the moment, I'm going to focus on asking more questions, rather than doling out unsolicited advice in our 1:1s. Could you please be mindful of whether you notice me doing that or not over the next 30 days.

When the 30 days are up, send out another quick email, Google form or, if you prefer, face to face. You can ask,

With regard to asking more questions, rather than doling out unsolicited advice in our 1:1s, what did you notice? Have things improved, stayed the same, or gotten worse? With regard to this goal, what suggestions do you have for me for the next 30 days?

And repeat.

Make it a habit for everyone, not just you

This approach not only serves to maintain momentum in the leader's development, but also serves as a useful evaluation tool as to whether or not any related coaching program has been impactful.

It also serves as an excellent strategy to embed the language and habits that we're exploring in this book throughout your organisation.

Once you have cycled through the process for several months, you can invite members of your learning team to start the process for themselves.

The learning team adopts exactly the same approach that you took.

Ask for feedback. Identify their learning goals. Enlist a learning team and cycle through the process.

Several months into it, they invite their learning teams to engage in the process.

We encourage people to be more receptive to feedback by creating an environment in which we seek theirs first. When they see that the process isn't some form of veiled performance management trap, many of the shortcomings of a traditional 360 process are avoided. When professionals see genuine learning, growth and development in the people around them, that's when people will want to engage in something that up until this point, they would probably rather avoid.

In the next chapter we explore the importance of psychological safety in the workplace. One of the most powerful ways a leader can create this is by modelling vulnerability and seeking out, then acting on, feedback from their team.

The sweet spot

After reading this chapter:

What new insight(s) do you have?

....

....

....

....

What new intention(s) do you have?

....

....

....

....

What action(s) will you start / stop / keep doing in order to enhance your leadership?

....

....

....

....

Chapter 6

MAKE IT SAFE TO STUFF UP

High performance is not about being perfect

This chapter in a nutshell

- you'll be introduced to the concept of psychological safety

- you'll be encouraged to reflect on the level of psychological safety in your team

- you'll learn how to develop higher levels of psychological safety in the teams you lead

Have you ever wondered what separates the best teams from the rest? Whether it's in the boardroom, school staffroom or even a professional sporting team's locker room, there's something that's even more important than talent when it comes to being the most effective team possible.

Get on the bus or you'll find yourself under it

'I've told them,' said Stephanie — very calmly — 'if I get called in to the boss over any of this, I'm throwing them all under the bus.'

I was working with a group of 16 middle leaders at a school in Sydney, and it was one of those moments when you sense that while everyone heard what was said, no-one quite believed what they'd heard.

To clarify what she meant, I offered Stephanie the opportunity to give us a little more context.

'That might have been the gist of what you said, but what words did you actually use?' I enquired.

Stephanie looked at me. 'Those exact words. Why should I pay for others' mistakes? They need to know there's a consequence if they don't do their job properly.'

Stephanie was responding to a question I had posed to the group about what happens if people make mistakes when part of a team, and whether or not some of her team members might feel mistakes are held against them, while others see mistakes as a normal part of operation and opportunities to learn.

As we dug into this, Stephanie explained that she was trying to make her team take more ownership of their work, in this case the formatting of an end-of-year examination. Over the past couple of years there had been quite a turnover in staff, and as less experienced staff took on more responsibilities, mistakes had started to creep into some areas of their work, but her way of trying to get everyone on the bus was to threaten them *with* the bus.

Is it safe here?

Have you ever found yourself in a meeting where you don't agree with the prevailing thinking? Or perhaps a decision's been made and you're not sure how or why, or even if that decision should have been made? But rather than speak up about it or speak up about your difference of opinion, you keep it to yourself until after the meeting and then you go and debrief with someone else. 'I can't believe they've gone and done that!' or 'I don't understand why they've done that'.

If this isn't you, maybe it's a colleague who comes to you after one of their meetings and says, 'You're not going to believe what they're doing now ...'

Or maybe you did speak up in a meeting and someone came to you afterwards and said, 'Oh, well said. We're all right behind you'. And you're left thinking, 'Well, why didn't you say that in the meeting?'

The phenomenon of not wanting to speak up about something even though it's really important is often a sign that there's a lack of psychological safety in an organisation or, more specifically, in a team or group of people.

In her book *The Fearless Organization*, Amy Edmondson defines psychological safety as 'a belief that no one will be punished or humiliated for speaking up with ideas, questions, concerns, or mistakes'.

When you're part of a team that needs to make decisions about complex issues but you feel your ideas will be shunned or that disagreeing with another idea will be held against you, you learn to keep those ideas and your thinking to yourself.

It's a self-preservation strategy. It's better to keep your head down than stick it up and get it shot off.

The problem with that is, lots of really good people and lots of really good ideas never get heard. Added to that, common thinking and common ways of doing things don't get challenged. And this can lead to all manner of issues, not the least of which being that teams simply don't perform at their best. They don't extract all the potential that's there.

My team and I are often invited into organisations by someone who says something along the lines of, 'We just want to get everyone on board', or 'We want our team to get the most out of themselves'. A lot of the time, we're talking about—and with—highly skilled people. Whether they're in the education, corporate or sporting world, we're dealing with people who are very good at what they do. What they sometimes struggle with is getting the best out of each other because of this lack of psychological safety.

If you feel that a mistake is going to be held against you, it's sensible not to take a risk, not to try something new—to play it safe. But when highly skilled people decide to start playing it safe, they plateau, and the performance that you might expect to get out of a group of high performers is nowhere near what it could and perhaps should be.

To put it simply, you can't have a high-performing team without a high level of psychological safety.

Let's revisit Amy Edmondson's definition of psychological safety.

To what extent do the teams you work in hold the belief that no-one will be punished or humiliated for speaking up with ideas, questions, concerns or mistakes?

To what extent is that actually true for you?

I invite you to consider the two statements below and the extent to which you can agree with them by indicating on a scale from 1 to 5 where:

1 = Strongly Disagree

2 = Disagree

3 = Neither Agree nor Disagree

4 = Agree

5 = Strongly Agree

It is safe to take a risk on your team.

| 1 | 2 | 3 | 4 | 5 |

Making a mistake on your team will not be held against you.

| 1 | 2 | 3 | 4 | 5 |

These two questions are from the psychological safety survey developed by Amy Edmondson. You can reflect on them from your own point of view, but I'd urge you to also put them out to your team using the tools available online at www.actofleadership.com.

Following the middle leader workshop I described at the start of this chapter, my colleague Tim Perkins and I were invited back to work with Stephanie's team. Perhaps unsurprisingly, the focus of our work was to enhance team dynamics. As part of our preliminary data-gathering we administered a survey that included the two statements above.

I want to share with you what happened when we asked Stephanie's team if they agreed or disagreed with the statement, *It is safe to take a risk on this team.*

However, instead of just asking to what extent they agreed or disagreed, we first asked them to identify what they would like their answer to be. That is, in an ideal world, what would they like to say? Of a team of 14 people, all 14 identified that they would like to say they strongly agree with the statement, which is probably to be expected (see figure 6.1, overleaf). It's hard to make a case against wanting to do that.

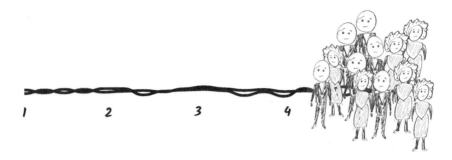

Figure 6.1: where Stephanie's team want to be

Yet, when we followed up with 'To what extent do you agree or disagree with the statement, *It is safe to take a risk on this team*' we found the results shown in figure 6.2.

Figure 6.2: where Stephanie's team actually are

We saw the distribution go from all 14 people wanting to be a 5 to only six of them being a 5, with some of them unable to commit either way for any number of reasons. Two of the team disagreed with that statement.

In total, only half of the team could agree that it is safe to take a risk on that team, despite all of them saying they want it to be safe to take a risk.

There are no solutions in that particular graphic, but it does provide a starting point for a series of conversations.

Why can't we all agree with that statement?

What constitutes a risk?

What is risky for us?

What's it like to be a 2?

What do we need to do more of for us all to be able to be a 5?

What do we need to do less of?

In some workplaces, speaking up is risky. In some cases, people fear for their job if they speak up, whereas in other organisations, that's just part of business as usual. The boss or team leader invites challenge. They want people to push back and challenge their thinking.

When you start hearing colleagues reflect on these questions you gain an insight into how and why they do what they do.

Let's have a look at the second statement: *Making a mistake on your team won't be held against you.*

This is an interesting statement to dig into as a team. In our experience of working with different groups, you can have a really good conversation about what this statement really means to people.

If your team is like the majority of teams we work with, no-one says they shouldn't be held accountable for their mistakes. In some ways it would be a sign of disrespect to not hold people accountable for their mistakes as that would suggest you don't expect much of them in the first place.

Yet people certainly recognise the difference between feeling they're being held accountable and feeling a mistake has been held against them. It's the feeling that something that happened six months, 12 months, maybe even two years ago, somehow keeps rearing its head in conversations or reviews, or when decisions about their involvement in projects seem to be prejudiced by something they thought had been dealt with.

Imagine for a second you lead a team that works in fear of making a mistake. How might that play out?

On the one hand, the less aware leader might consider that to be a good thing. They might misconstrue the motivation to not make a mistake with the motivation to raise standards. The irony here is that in order to raise standards, more often than not we need to venture into new territory, to do things we haven't done before, to challenge what we take for granted and in a very real sense be ready to make mistakes. But this fear of speaking up about—or making—mistakes only serves to stymie growth.

When I spoke to Amy Edmondson for my *Habits of Leadership* podcast we explored that while Instagram memes extoll the virtue of mistakes and the potential of learning from them, in reality, she says, 'Not too many of us are really enthusiastic about raising our hand to say, "Hey, look at the mistake I just made. Isn't this an interesting one? We can learn from it!"'

This is compounded when speaking up about *anything*—let alone a mistake—is seen as risky because we are, Edmondson explains, Spontaneous Image Managers. 'We care very much about the impressions others have of us and we unconsciously and consciously manage those at all times. And so, the reality is you could just draw a line and say, here's the threshold. Above this line I'll certainly speak immediately. Below this line, maybe it's a judgement call. And below this line over here, I wouldn't dream of saying it at work'.

What would your thresholds look like? What would you speak up about? What would you be hesitant about? And what would you absolutely not speak up about, even if you know it to be important?

I'm happy to speak up about this:

....

....

....

....

I'd think twice about speaking up about this (even though I consider it to be important):

....

....

....

....

I'd absolutely not speak up about this (even though I consider it to be important):

....

....

....

....

Now take a moment to consider why.

Why won't you speak up about important issues?

....

....

....

....

There are many things that should be said at work—perhaps by you, and almost certainly by your colleagues and team members—that could avoid all manner of issues ranging from safety failures to business losses. Edmondson told me, 'By increasing psychological safety, we could have more innovation and more inclusion. There's a lot of different outputs that we care about that we lose out on when we hold back'.

A canary in the coalmine could be to ask how comfortable are you, or the group as a whole, brainstorming ideas in front of each other?

Do team members always preface whatever they say with, 'Oh, this is probably a silly idea', or 'Maybe this is a silly question', as a qualifier before they say something?

Even though those qualifiers seem insignificant, and they're almost so commonly said as to go unheard, it just happens. People say them all the time.

Why?

There's a reason why people feel they need to qualify themselves before they ask a question or provide an idea. And that reason could be because they're worried about making a mistake or looking silly in front of other people.

Another indicator to look for is how much feedback people ask for and how much they give. And I'm not just talking about the traditional institutional feedback, 360 feedback or an observation that might form part of our annual process.

I'm talking about in general, how often does somebody say, 'Hey, can you come in and have a look at what I'm doing and tell me what you think?' Or, 'This is what I've put together. Can you give me some ideas on what I can do to improve it?'

How many times last month did people come to you and give you unsolicited feedback? I'm not talking about merely criticism or empty platitudes. I'm talking about real, authentic, useful feedback.

How many times did you seek out or give informal feedback?

If that isn't happening outside of the formal feedback pathways, it's a possible indicator that psychological safety might not be as high as it could be, or as you'd like it to be in order to get more out of your team.

I'm going as far as to say if you don't have psychological safety, you don't have a team. You just have a group of people who happen to work at the same place.

In view of the above, to what extent do you feel the need to enhance psychological safety in your team?

The Act of Leadership:
Be vulnerable

From the outset it's important to recognise that you don't need to be the big boss in order to enhance the psychological safety of your team. It might be easier if you are, but it's certainly not a requirement. You might choose to use a survey tool, or you might wish to ask your team members to reflect on statements similar to the ones I shared earlier. Of course, there's something of an irony here in that you probably need a degree of psychological safety in order to get these kinds of conversations going, and being more mindful of how we're showing up can be a good start.

For example, being aware of your body language and how you're sitting in a meeting, or whether or not you've got your laptop open or your phone on the table. Would you be somewhat distracted by those things? (Spoiler alert: Yes, you would be.)

You might not think anything of it, and you might be incredibly busy, but to the person talking or looking to you for guidance, not appearing interested in what they have to say starts to chip away at their psychological safety.

You can also start enhancing psychological safety by accepting that you need to demonstrate a level of vulnerability yourself. For example, do you ever talk about times when you made a mistake? If so, what did you learn from that experience? By modelling what we want to see in our team we're more likely to start seeing it.

Work hard to demonstrate engagement in meetings, whether it's through active listening or asking questions that demonstrate curiosity.

Even when things have gone completely awry, show up with a good Red/Blue balance and avoid placing blame on individuals or small groups. Rather, be sure to use inclusive language like, 'What do we need to do to ensure we learn from this down the track?'

Now, I can't believe I'm going to say this, but as well as body language, we need to be mindful of our facial expressions. I didn't realise this was such an issue, but over the past few years we've had more than a dozen leaders (yes, we keep a tally) articulate the need to work on their RBF (resting bitch face). Their words, not mine! And not exclusively females either!

One strategy we've come up with that seems to eradicate RBF is to nod your head to demonstrate agreement or understanding.

Of course, RBF is a condition you might not be aware you're afflicted with, so best to nod along just in case!

I'm constantly fascinated by how groups work in meetings, and we dig into this more deeply in chapter 10, but for now suffice to say, these meetings cannot, and should not, only be about the processes of business. Leaders should be diligent in ensuring that not only are meetings about the work that needs to be done, but they are also opportunities for the people and teams who need to do the work to become stronger. Too often, in our efforts to be more efficient and streamlined, we get straight down to business and interpersonal moments are lost, and in the worst cases meetings can serve to weaken a team dynamic, so it's important for leaders to demonstrate inclusiveness by making time for ad-hoc 1:1 chats, or coaching chats.

Make sure in group sessions to express gratitude when someone makes a contribution, especially if it is challenging or tackling a tough issue. And spend time finding out about team members' lives outside of their professional roles and responsibilities.

One workshop activity we like to facilitate when working with a group for the first time is the CPC.

The CPC requires team members to share with the group the name of a Champion, recall a Peak Experience from their life and discuss a Challenge that they've had to overcome. Sometimes we throw in an H: share a Hope they have for the future.

We've done this with all manner of groups—from corporate executives to schoolteachers to NRL footballers—and without fail, there are tears and there is a strong sense of empathy that builds from learning about the people you spend most of your working hours alongside.

The order of the CPC is important. By starting with the Champion and working around the group before progressing to the Peak Experience, you're able to build a level of trust in the group through sharing. By the time people get to the Challenge, even some of the most combative groups we've worked with are sharing. Of course, nobody is forced to share if they don't wish to, but in all the years of running it, we've never had anyone refuse to share.

You might be reading this thinking, 'Dan, mate, I don't have the time or the inclination to get into that sort of stuff'. If that's the case, I'd urge you to consider the time you spend dealing with drama, and how by investing the time here you might not need to spend all your time dealing with issues down the track.

So, if you're inclined and you can give it the time, it's a good idea to think about your own responses as you can lead off each section.

Take a moment to think, what would you share?

Who is your Champion and why? How have they championed you? How did they advocate for you? How have they supported, or challenged you to get where you are today?

....

....

....

....

What is a Peak Experience of your life? Why did you choose this event? What impact has it had on you?

....

....

....

....

What is a significant Challenge you've had to overcome? What made this particularly challenging for you? What did you learn from this?

....

....

....

....

And while I've got you, what's a Hope you have for the future? What are you doing to make this a reality?

....

....

....

....

Back to Stephanie and her team, and making it safe to take risks.

You'll remember that half of Stephanie's team said they didn't feel safe to take a risk on their team. You'll also remember that this is the same team that Stephanie had told—in no uncertain terms—that if she got called in to explain any mistakes, she would throw the team under the bus.

Building a sense of psychological safety in the group to a point where they could share openly took a bit of time. As you can imagine, the threat of the bus had taught them to keep their heads down, but, through a series of workshops, readings and even a short video from me on the matter, we were able to get to a point where the group could talk about what was needed in order for them to feel safer taking a risk.

These workshops, readings and videos included some of the points outlined above, as well as continually highlighting that the whole group had said they wanted it to be safe to take a risk on the team.

It's a powerful moment when you show a team what they want, highlight where they're at, and then work side by side with them to bridge the gap.

The key conversation to establishing new norms to develop psychological safety centres on two questions:

- What do I need that I'm not currently getting from this group?

- What do I need to give that I'm not currently giving to this group?

When you start hearing your colleagues say things like, 'I need to know I'm valued and respected', 'I need my colleagues to assume my intentions are positive' and 'I need to know that asking questions is seen as a strength, not a weakness', it's impossible for the team to continue operating as it did previously.

It's even more powerful when your colleagues start sharing what they can give that they're not currently giving. We often—but not always—ask this question after we've heard what our colleagues need. In the case of Stephanie's team we heard:

'I need to give others my full attention.'

'I need to give my time to let others be heard rather than rushing to decisions I think are right.'

'I need to give more autonomy for people to work how they would like to work.'

118

As you can tell, it takes time to create a space where people feel comfortable opening up to this level of vulnerability, but an investment of time here will free up the time you will almost definitely spend dealing with dysfunction down the track.

We talk more in chapter 12 about how to hold each other accountable to these new insights, but for now, take a moment to consider:

What do you need from your team that you're not currently getting?

....

....

....

....

What does your team need from you that you're not currently giving?

....

....

....

....

THE ACT OF LEADERSHIP

The sweet spot

After reading this chapter:

What new insight(s) do you have?

....

....

....

....

What new intention(s) do you have?

....

....

....

....

What action(s) will you start / stop / keep doing in order to enhance your leadership?

....

....

....

....

Chapter 7

LESS CARROT, LESS STICK

Find out what makes people tick

This chapter in a nutshell

- you'll see why traditional approaches to motivation miss the mark

- you'll be introduced to Self-Determination Theory as a means to motivate your team

- you'll be encouraged to view motivation through the lens of authentic engagement, rather than merely ensuring people are doing their jobs

According to their website, Gallup is a global analytics and advice firm that has been in business for over 80 years and who 'know more about the will of employees, customers, students and citizens than anyone in the world'.

That's a pretty bold claim, but then again, they base this claim on having over 35 million respondents to their engagement surveys.

Gallup is engaged, to some degree, by 90 per cent of the Fortune 500 companies, and they are trusted by leaders across the globe to inform and advise on leadership and workplace engagement matters.

Each year they conduct employee workplace engagement surveys around the world and share their findings.

Gallup defines engaged employees as those who are involved in, enthusiastic about and committed to their work and workplace.

In 2018, the last time they shared findings for Australia and New Zealand, Gallup reported only 14 per cent of Australian and New Zealand workers reported feeling this way.

Fourteen per cent! I don't use exclamation marks very often, but I feel it's warranted here.

So what about the rest?

According to Gallup, 15 per cent of Aussie and Kiwi workers were actively disengaged, meaning employees aren't just unhappy at work—they are resentful that their needs aren't being met and are acting out their unhappiness.

More employees are actively disengaged than engaged.

But the majority of workers aren't engaged or actively disengaged, they're somewhere between these two poles.

They're what Gallup describe as merely not engaged. They're not causing major dramas for you as those who are actively disengaged are, but they're certainly not as effective as they might be. Those employees who are not engaged, according to Gallup, are those who 'May be generally satisfied but are not cognitively and emotionally connected to their work and workplace; they will usually show up to work and do the minimum required but will quickly leave their company for a slightly better offer'.

By way of comparison, Australian and New Zealand workplaces appear to be similar in this regard to others around the world, with the exception of the United States, which, according to Gallup, outperforms pretty much every other country. Over the past 20 years, the percentage of engaged workers in the US workforce has averaged approximately 30 per cent.

If you had to take a guess, what proportion of your team or organisation would fall into each of Gallup's categories?

Actively engaged: engaged employees are those who are involved in, enthusiastic about and committed to their work and workplace.

Percentage: _____ %

Who are some good examples of people who fall into this category?

....

....

....

....

Not engaged: not engaged employees may be generally satisfied but are not cognitively and emotionally connected to their work and workplace; they will usually show up to work and do the minimum required but will quickly leave their company for a slightly better offer.

Percentage: _____ %

Who are some good examples of people who fall into this category? (You don't need to list them all!)

....

....

....

....

Actively disengaged: actively disengaged employees are not only unhappy at work but are also resentful that their needs aren't being met and are acting out their unhappiness.

Percentage: _____ %

Who are some good (if that's the right word here!) examples of people who fall into this category?

....

....

....

....

As a leader, what do you make of those percentages? Bearing in mind all we've learned about cognitive biases and mindset, we shouldn't put too much weight on them right now, other than to ask a question:

Do you think there is an opportunity to enhance engagement in your workplace?

If so, read on.

If not: Seriously? Why are you still reading this book? Surely there's something on Netflix you could be watching.

Understanding engagement

As well as Gallup, many other people have defined engagement, including me.

I define engagement as:

> the sense of living life high on energy, curiosity and absorption. Engaged individuals pursue goals with determination and vitality.

You can see how this has a good synergy with Gallup's definition, but my definition deliberately considers engagement outside of work as well. You could equally apply my definition to work, hobbies, sport or relationships.

So with these two definitions in mind, let's dig into it.

For many years, when organisations have wanted to motivate people to behave in a certain way, they have leaned heavily on the use of extrinsic motivation.

The carrot-and-stick approach

You've likely used this approach to motivate people yourself, and you've certainly had people attempt to motivate you by using carrots and sticks. If you're a parent, chances are you use them every day to get your kids to do what's needed.

Every. Single. Day. Which in itself should give you an insight into the effectiveness (or lack thereof) of using extrinsic motivators when trying to effect long-term behaviour change or buy-in. Yet we still see organisations using such approaches in their attempts to motivate people. In the corporate world, we might pay someone a bit more, or promise a bonus if they meet certain targets, while in schools, the threat of punishments or the promise of 'Student of the Week' awards are used as ways to motivate students (and parents and teachers!).

Of course, extrinsic motivators play an important role. I mean, as much as I would do my job for free, the bank unfortunately doesn't accept 'good vibes' as a form of mortgage repayment, so being compensated for my work is important.

However, if we only have extrinsic motivators—if I only did my job for the money—then my level of engagement, motivation and likely performance would not be as high over the long term as that of someone else who is operating with a higher degree of intrinsic motivation.

If what you're being asked to do is in sync with what makes you tick, then you'll rarely need a nudge to do extra. More likely you'll need to look out for your wellbeing, as in some cases intrinsically motivated people can be susceptible to burnout.

A simple way to start thinking about this is to consider what elements of your work you have to do, but if you had the choice, you wouldn't?

Then compare this with the elements of your work that you want to do, and that you would want to do even if you didn't have to.

Me: How do these elements compare? Do you find yourself working in the way you want to, or in the way you have to?

You: It depends.

Me: *On what? How does that play out?*

You:

....

....

....

....

Once you've established this for yourself, consider the level of confidence you'd have in exploring these elements for the people you listed above in each of Gallup's categories.

Being able to do this is a sign that you're starting to understand what makes your people tick. And if you start to understand this, then you can start to help them engage more at work.

You: But it's about them! Why won't they just do their job?

Me: Because it's not about them. It's about *us*.

I've never worked with an organisation for whom the 'us and them' phenomenon isn't an issue on some level. If it's not between the leadership team and those lower down the organisation chart, then it's between the regional leadership and national leadership teams, or between sales and marketing departments, or the software designers and the engineers.

Of course, it's normal human behaviour to find and identify with a particular group or tribe, but as a leader you must remain vigilant that the 'us and them' mentality doesn't creep into how you view issues around engagement.

When employees disengage, it isn't their problem. It's ours. *They* don't need to fix things. *We* need to fix things. *Together.*

This can be unpalatable for many leaders when I raise it, but again, I urge you to adopt a growth mindset. At the very least we can approach this with a degree of curiosity to see why it is you haven't been able to engage your team or colleagues as well as you might.

We need more tribes

We explored in the last chapter the importance of psychological safety in teams. In fact, I went as far to say that you can't have a high performing team without psychological safety.

One of the core elements that bridges the concepts of psychological safety and engagement is the sense of belonging.

When we work with organisations or teams, we conceptualise belonging as the foundation upon which we will lay the necessary pillars of engagement.

To what extent do your team feel part of the tribe?

Do they know you have their back?

Do they feel able to be themselves, and can they bring up tough issues without fear of being kicked out of the tribe?

The extent to which an individual feels part of the team is an excellent indicator as to the level of impact they'll seek to have. Members of your team who don't feel a sense of belonging or camaraderie will likely gravitate to the fringes, both literally and metaphorically. They'll sit outside of the circle. They'll engage only when directed to, or only offer ideas when put on the spot to do so.

Team members on the periphery rarely go above and beyond, and almost never turn in their best performance.

If you're a sports fan, you can likely think of a player in a team you follow who doesn't appear to 'fit in'. How do their performances, both on and off the field, compare to other players who do appear to belong?

By way of further illustration, I want to share with you a story about one of the most successful teams of all time. The New Zealand All Blacks rugby union team.

Before I start, if I were to ask you what is the first thing you think of when I say, 'The All Blacks', I imagine the word 'haka' would come to mind fairly quickly.

The haka is a traditional dance in Maori culture, and since around 1905, the All Blacks have routinely performed it just prior to kick-off in international matches. The haka is so intertwined with All Black folklore that it would be hard to imagine an All Black team not wanting to perform it.

However, many people are surprised when they learn that in the early 2000s this became a very real proposition. Members of the team were growing tired of the pre-game ritual. This weariness had come about due to the players losing connection with and understanding of what it represented. In his book *Legacy*, James Kerr writes of how Gilbert Enoka, the All Blacks manager, told him the senior players were fed up with the TV cameras being shoved in their faces, and besides, the haka was for Maoris, and many of the All Black Squad at that time were not Maori.

In fact, Enoka goes as far as to say, 'We were close to losing the whole thing'.

Imagine that? Something so ingrained and yet so close to being lost. Something that TV broadcasters, sponsors and fans expect to see.

Consider what might happen if—in your workplace—your people started to resent something that was ingrained in your culture.

It might play out in a number of ways, not least the possibility that they would be told to 'just do your job'. Or 'We've always done it this way', 'Get on with it' or 'If you don't like it, leave'.

The All Blacks, however, took a different path. They listened.

At the time, coach Graham Henry—since knighted for his services to New Zealand sport—recognised that the current crop of New Zealand test players had every reason to feel disconnected from the Ka Mate Haka that was regularly performed. After all, it stemmed from Maori tradition. But as Henry noted, 'It's not just Maori and European...the All Blacks team is made up of Tongan, Samoan, Fijian, as well as Maori and European'.

Henry and the playing group decided that a new haka was needed. One that reflected the diverse nature of the playing group and New Zealand society and one that the players could reconnect with and authentically 'live' the meaning of.

With the assistance of a Maori tohunga (wise man) who was also a dance performer, the All Blacks sat down and had many conversations about culture, metaphor and language before choreographing a brand new haka.

This haka became known as the Kapa o Pango and is reserved for big occasions such as Bledisloe Cup matches or World Cup semi-finals and the like.

The approach that the All Blacks took is one I encourage all leaders to consider.

Often, we think that the people need to fit into the culture. But for me, the most effective cultures invite people in, but then adapt to ensure they feel like they belong. If they belong, they stay and they grow, not only as individuals, but also in their teams and the culture.

Once we've laid the foundation of belonging, we can then look to build the pillars of authentic engagement.

I use Self-Determination Theory with leaders to help them see how they can do this.

Self-Determination Theory (SDT) grew out of the work of psychologists Richard Ryan and Edward Deci, who first introduced their ideas in their 1985 book *Intrinsic Motivation and Self-Determination in Human Behavior*. They developed a theory of motivation which suggested that people tend to be driven by a need to grow and gain fulfilment. Ryan and Deci explained that for a human to be authentically engaged or intrinsically motivated to do something, they needed a sense of three things: autonomy, competence and relatedness. Daniel Pink later wrote about SDT in some detail in his book *Drive: The surprising truth about what motivates us*. He built on Ryan and Deci's work and used the words 'mastery' and 'purpose' in place of 'competence' and 'relatedness'. If you haven't read it, you should. (Just finish this book first.)

Let's explore each of these pillars.

Autonomy: we want to be in the driver's seat

Have you ever been sitting in traffic on the way home from work? The cars are backed up, and everything is moving at a snail's pace. As much as you try to peer down the line of vehicles, you can't see what's causing the delay, all the while Google Maps is doing that non-committal thing of showing your route in amber. There's no electronic signage or item in the news on the radio to explain what's going on. It's been a long day and you just want to get home. Your mood isn't improved when a motorcyclist screams up the breakdown lane or (worse!) weaves in between lanes, somehow managing to dodge each and every wing mirror as they do so. You have no idea where they're going; all you do know is they'll be there before you get home. You imagine them smirking to themselves smugly as they do it. And they annoy you. A lot.

Actually, let's hold up for a second.

You see, it's not the traffic, the lack of information or the bikie per se that's annoying you.

Rather it's the loss of control.

You suddenly lack agency and volition. You're stuck. At the whim of some, while others pass you by.

So, as soon as you can, you turn off. Even though you never turn off here, tonight you do. You ask Google Maps to navigate and it tells you it will likely add another 5–10 minutes to your journey. But you do it.

You're willing—in fact you want—to spend longer in the car (remember that's what started this whole thing) in return for exerting some control over the situation. It was your choice to turn off. That's how important having a sense of autonomy, agency or volition is to us.

Side note: It's also for this reason that people panic-buy toilet rolls during a pandemic. They can't control the health of the human race, but they can grab a month's supply of loo paper, dammit.

So let's consider that a lot of the time, when we talk about the work in an organisation, the focus tends to be on what's in it for others? What's in it for the organisation?, What's in it for our customers? or What's in it for our students?

All very important questions obviously, but in order to enhance intrinsic motivation, we need to explore what's in it for the people doing the work. Over and above monetary compensation, how does the work resonate with their core values?

How does this give them more volition in their work?

Competence/mastery: it's hard to be motivated when we suck

We discussed previously how not feeling at least competent in any given scenario can lead to anxiety. In SDT the point is made that when we do feel competent and feel we can strive for mastery without the fear of failure or judgement, we are more likely to feel intrinsically motivated.

Nowhere in your life is this more evident than in the world of gaming.

Whether we're playing 'Call of Duty' or 'Candy Crush', it's the sense of competence and mastery that keeps bringing us back. Game designers have been able to create feedback-rich worlds where at any given point, a gamer (you or your child) can answer these two questions:

- What are you doing well?

- What might go wrong?

And when things do go wrong, they can answer these questions:

- What went wrong?

- What will you do better next time?

- When will you get the chance to do better next time?

Here's the point:

We give up playing games when they become too easy.

We have an innate desire to be stretched.

However, somewhere along the line, probably because of our over-reliance on carrots and sticks, we've created a society in education and the workplace where many people have learned to give up when things get too hard—because you'll cop the stick—so they pursue the things they find easy in order to feast on carrots. That's how you play that game.

Indeed, I contend this is one of the main reasons we tend to confuse compliance for engagement. We see people who are doing what they're supposed to be doing. They're doing what they've been told, and we tell ourselves they're engaged.

And look, they might be. But there is also a fair chance they're just playing the game. They've realised that compliance is enough.

Let's go back to my conceptualisation of authentic engagement:

> the sense of living life high on energy, curiosity and absorption. Engaged individuals pursue goals with determination and vitality.

Do your people pursue their professional goals with determination and vitality?

As a result of achieving their KPIs, do they actually feel they've grown not only as professionals but also as human beings?

Or do they view them as boxes to be ticked, and do they do just enough to keep people off their back?

Your answers to these questions will go a long way to explaining levels of motivation in your team.

(So what are your answers?)

....

....

....

....

Relatedness/purpose: what's the point?

In Ryan and Deci's original work they cited relatedness as being a fundamental requirement for people to be intrinsically motivated.

They define relatedness as:

> the development and maintenance of close personal relationships such as best friends and romantic partners as well as belonging to groups.

The simple point here is that in order for me to feel intrinsically motivated, I need to have a sense of belonging. I need to feel I'm part of the tribe and you have my best interests at heart. You can no doubt recall a time when you didn't have that sense. I wonder if you can recall a time when others in your company might not have felt part of your tribe. How might that have affected their behaviour?

In Pink's application of SDT he also talks about purpose. As well as a sense of belonging, autonomy and competence/mastery, Pink argues individuals require a real sense of why they're doing something.

You'll see resonance in the next chapter between this and the importance of truly communicating an organisational vision.

Interestingly, when I interviewed Pink for my *Habits of Leadership* podcast, we were discussing his notion of purpose and he said that if he had his time again, he would make the distinction between what he called 'little p' purpose and 'Big P' purpose.

'Big P' purpose refers to grand gestures of changing the world.

'Little p' purpose refers to smaller gestures that provide the *why*: 'We're working hard to make the best sandwich we can because workers who come here for lunch need to have the best experience we can provide for them'.

He told me of a study in which an assistant professor at University College London set up four scenarios in a real cafeteria for two weeks. In the first, diners and cooks couldn't view one another; in the second, the diners could see the cooks; in the third, the cooks could see the diners; and in the fourth, both the diners and the cooks were visible to one another.

The researchers timed the preparation and conducted surveys about the service and food. The results showed that when the cooks could see their patrons, the food quality got higher ratings. Ryan Buell from Harvard Business School set up the experiment and he suggests that seeing the customer can make employees feel more appreciated, more satisfied with their jobs and more willing to exert effort. It's important to note that it wasn't just the perception of quality that improved—the food objectively got better. During the experiment they had an observer in the kitchen taking notes and timing service. Normally, chefs would make eggs on the grill in advance, adding them to plates as needed and often overcooking them. When the chefs saw the customers, they started making eggs to order more often.

In our work, we've taken Ryan and Deci's work, and that of Pink, in order to conceptualise the conditions we see as being important for leaders to think about. Figure 7.1 shows how we conceptualise this.

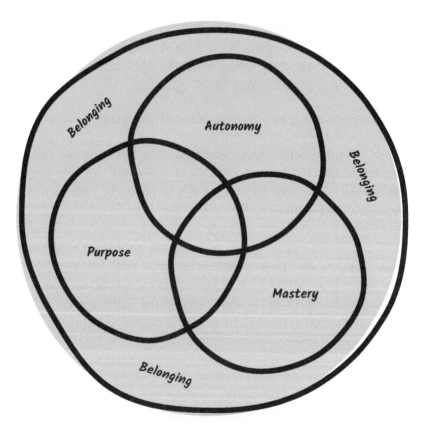

Figure 7.1: leaders must build the pillars of SDT on a foundation of belonging

The Act of Leadership: Understand what makes you and your team tick

When are you most engaged? When can you recognise you have all three pillars of SDT built on the foundation of belonging?

....

....

....

....

Can you recognise what you do in order to build this for your team?

....

....

....

....

How might people feel if one or more of these elements are missing? Feel free to add your own thoughts to the table on the next page.

Requirements of authentic engagement				Result
Belonging	Autonomy	Mastery	Purpose	Engagement ....
	Autonomy	Mastery	Purpose	Unsafe ....
Belonging		Mastery	Purpose	Compliant ....
Belonging	Autonomy		Purpose	Frustration ....
Belonging	Autonomy	Mastery		Aimless ....

The sweet spot

After reading this chapter:

What new insight(s) do you have?

....

....

....

....

What new intention(s) do you have?

....

....

....

....

What action(s) will you start / stop / keep doing in order to enhance your leadership?

....

....

....

....

Chapter 8

BE BETTER AT CHANGE

Stop trying to get people on the bus

This chapter in a nutshell

- you'll be introduced to a simple framework with which to view organisational change

- you'll learn the importance of authentically communicating the change vision

- you'll learn how to empower your team to drive the change initiative, rather than resist it

Think of a time when an attempt at organisational change failed.

If you're sitting there thinking, 'I can't, because everything my company or team has ever tried, we've just smashed it out of the park. I'm afraid I have no frame of reference', then feel free to skip this chapter.

If, however, one or more instances of failed change attempts spring to mind, take a moment to jot down the reasons—as you see them—for the failure.

Some reasons will have had a more significant impact than others, but if you feel they contributed to the failure then include them.

Jot down as many reasons for failed change attempts as you can think of.

....

....

....

....

Now, if you're like most people I meet, despite your experience with failed change attempts, you'll likely back yourself to lead it better this time. And I'm sure you will—and this chapter is designed to complement your efforts by helping you avoid making the same mistakes you made in the past.

I'm going to share with you a simple model for discussing change. I came across it a few years back and have used it extensively with publicly listed companies and schools to help them improve the manner in which they implement change initiatives. It was developed by Tim Knoster, Richard Villa and Jacqueline Thousand. The model, as outlined in figure 8.1, gives us a useful lens through which to look at system change because it proposes five elements that must be in place in order for change to be effective. It also highlights some of the possible outcomes should any of the elements be missing. You might find this illuminating when you look back at your own list of reasons for why change failed.

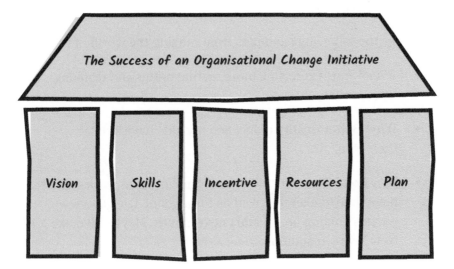

Figure 8.1: Knoster, Villa and Thousand's pillars of organisational change

Let's look at each in turn.

Vision: what, why – and crucially – why now?

'What's your vision?' A question that, while I have no verifiable data to back me up, I would suggest is asked hundreds if not thousands of times across the globe every single day.

As overused as this term may appear to be, when it comes to change, the importance of communicating the vision cannot be overstated. It simply has to happen or else change won't happen. In essence the vision is the *what, why* and *why now?*

It's obvious to see why people need to know the *what* and the *why*. What's less obvious to many is the importance of communicating the *why now* aspect of the vision.

Without *why now*, efforts at change, either large or small, are affected by a lack of urgency.

Consider the following examples from outside the world of work:

- *What?* Start exercising more, eating better and drinking less alcohol.

- *Why?* Better quality of life. See my kids have kids of their own.

- *Why now?* Oh, I can't do it now. I'm flat out at work. I don't have time to exercise. And as for alcohol, I've got a few parties coming up. I'll start next month. Maybe I'll make it a New Year's resolution.

or

- *What?* Reduce our reliance on fossil fuels.

- *Why?* Science.

- *Why now?* Woah, I'm not getting an electric car mate. And I kinda like my air conditioning unit to make it chilly in summer. Besides, no point if others aren't doing their bit.

Without the *why now* there's no need to change. There's no sense of urgency. In his excellent book *Leading Change*, John Kotter describes complacency (the lack of urgency) as the enemy of change. He goes as far as to say that creating a sense of urgency is the most important step in the change process.

Take a moment to call to mind a change you want to make, either on an organisational level, or regarding how you operate as a leader. Take a moment to jot down your 3Ws.

My change

What?

....

Why?

....

Why now?

....

Having taken time to write this down, it should be fairly easy to communicate it to anyone else who needs to be aware of it.

However, what I find interesting is that the manner in which people go about communicating the vision often misses the mark, and people end up sitting across the table from me saying, 'But I've explained it to them. Why can't they all get on board? Why don't they get it?'

What we have here is ... failure to communicate

I've never studied Latin, but I'm always interested to learn where the words we use today come from. In this case, the word 'communication' comes from the Latin *communicare*, which means 'to share, or to make common'.

Can you think of a time when you got the wrong end of the stick? Maybe someone said something to you, but because their use of language was not common to you, or you both didn't share the same understanding of what was being said, you became confused?

For example, imagine my confusion when the first time I was in a department store in Australia, having recently moved from Manchester in the UK, I was casually perusing the menswear section when over the PA system I heard, 'Can someone from Manchester come to the customer service desk please? Anyone from Manchester?'

Now, while readers from outside Australia might find it unusual that a department store would want to meet with a shopper from 17 000 kilometres away (as I did), only Australian readers will immediately understand where the confusion arises. As it turns out, in Australia, and for reasons I can't quite figure out, manchester refers to bed linen. 'Can someone from Bed linen come to the customer service desk please?' Well why didn't you just say that?

Imagine my reaction when in my first teaching job here in Australia, when I was taking a group of Year 10 students to the beach, I asked my head of department what they would wear. 'Well, thongs for starters, obviously.' (We call them flip flops in England, and thongs are certainly not appropriate for school!)

I have a friend from the UK who, when she was asked to 'bring a plate' to a party, did just that.

No food to share. Just a plate.

The point is, even though we all speak the same language, we might also speak with different understandings. If we don't take the time to explore this space, then the true vision will be misunderstood, confusing or in some cases lost altogether.

The kicker here, of course, is that—if we think back to chapter 6—if your team lack the psychological safety to speak up, then they will always opt to keep quiet and remain confused, rather than seek clarification and risk looking stupid.

And when confusion reigns, humans like to fill in the blanks. When we don't know why we're doing something, we come up with reasons for why we're doing things. How many times, in response to the question 'Why are we doing this?' have you heard:

'Dunno, she must have been at a conference.'

'It's the latest fad; don't worry, keep your head down, it'll pass.'

'He's just building his CV isn't he?'

The confusion comes about because typically, we overestimate our ability to communicate the importance of the vision, while at the same time underestimate the amount of time it will take us to communicate a vision.

As the leader, you have the vision. You know what we should be doing, and you know why we should be doing it, and you know why we should be doing it now. Perhaps it's been consuming you for months because you've seen what's on the horizon, perhaps you've spent sleepless nights over it. At the very least you've given it a whole lot more thought than your team.

So, if you spend an hour with a flashy PowerPoint presentation and tell other people the vision, can you really expect that they'll get on board?

Too many leaders mistake *articulating* the vision with communicating the vision, and what they miss is the need—and indeed the opportunity—for people to push back and question.

People need to get it in their own language and have the time to clarify their own understanding and meaning.

Why do we expect to be able to communicate to a group the importance of our vision in a fraction of the time it took us to realise its importance?

In some cases, it's taken us our whole professional career to get to this point. Yet we're expecting to be able to dictate to somebody else, 'Oh no, this is the new thing, you need to get on board'.

In schools it could be a new way of teaching; in a business it could be a new software program; in a sporting team it could be a new positional play. After considerable time and thought, you're at the point where you can say, 'Oh yeah, something needs to be tweaked. This is the change we're going to make. This is the new thing we're going to do'.

We assume that others are seeing what we're seeing, and if they're not, they'll see it as soon as we talk them through it with a PowerPoint.

They won't.

Skills: the how

But imagine for a second that as a leader you have managed to effectively communicate the vision and your people have an authentic shared understanding of the *what, why* and *why now*. Great job.

However if the second pillar of Knoster, Villa and Thousand's framework is missing then we hit problems. If people feel they don't have the necessary skills to execute on the vision they get anxious. As explored in chapter 2, anxiety is perfectly normal due to the Red mind looking out for us. But left unchecked, you'll remember, it can lead us to behaving in ways that affect not only ourselves, but those around us.

It feels safer to do the old thing well rather than the new thing badly.

The way we speak about change in organisations is often problematic. We might talk about the early adopters in reverential terms, while those who are a little slower to catch on are just dragging their heels.

It's not unusual to hear pejorative terms used to describe people who resist change, and this says to the people struggling with change that they are no longer good enough and what they do is no longer good enough. You'll remember from our discussions around mindset, for some it's not just what they do that's being threatened, but in some cases it's their whole sense of identity. If these people feel they lack the capability to do what they're being asked to do and don't see any roadmap to enhance their skills, they get anxious.

Our old favourite, Red mind, takes over and puts them into fight, flight and freeze mode, not only when they're at work, but any time they think about work.

And so, rather than expose themselves, they may start to arc up against the boss or the company, claiming everything is a union issue or argue that, 'This new approach is wrong, that's the problem—it's not me!' Alternatively, they might choose to keep their head down and hope that nobody spots what they're doing (or not doing!). They might just check out: cognitively—or literally—remove themselves from the situation.

This can happen with people who understand the *what*, the *why*, and the *why now*, and in some cases, that ups the stakes because they know why this is important. They know why we should be doing it now, but they feel they can't so that actually makes them even more anxious. It's a vicious spiral.

So. Without vision, we get confusion. Without skills, we get anxiety.

Okay, next.

Incentive: what's in it for me?

Picture the scene. You've done a remarkable job of taking the time to communicate the vision, and you've taken the time to ensure that people have the skills to execute on the vision and if they haven't got the skills they can see a clearly mapped-out way to gain them without feeling that it's being held against them. As a result they are neither confused nor anxious, but every now and then you come across someone who, despite knowing the *what*, the *why* and the *why now,* and who possesses the skills to do what's required, simply doesn't want to. When we fail to tap into the motivations of our people, we encounter resistance.

We spent the last chapter exploring what it takes for people to be intrinsically motivated, and we examined the role that having a sense of belonging, autonomy, mastery and purpose plays in creating environments in which people are more likely to be authentically engaged. You can see how purpose and mastery relate directly to vision and skills respectively.

It's important to create a sense of belonging and autonomy within the change initiative itself so leaders can avoid that well-worn cliché of change being done *to* people. If people feel part of the new thing, and they have some agency about how they can approach it, then they are more likely to feel as though they are driving the new initiative and change is being done *with them*, as opposed to *to them*.

Resources: what's this going to take?

I talk about the three important resources being time, money and space. Without adequate resourcing, not only does change not take place, but worse, your best people leave.

Let me illustrate why.

Imagine as a leader you've done an incredible job communicating the vision, and people have a shared understanding of the *what*, the *why* and the *why now*. Some of these people also have the skills to make a quick and effective start on the change initiative, and better still? They bloody well want to!

But then, just as they start getting into it, they realise that not enough (or in some cases, any) time, money or space has been put aside for their work. This is when good people get frustrated. And if you've done your job well and achieved the first three pillars, really frustrated, and they start to look around for places where time, money and space is put aside for such efforts.

And that really does sting. You've done all the hard work of getting the buy-in. You've got them on the bus, only for them to go and jump onto a better bus down the road.

It's not about more, it's about how

I've lost count of the number of times people have said to me, 'Yeah Dan, that would be great, but we simply don't have any more money, time or space', leading to cultures where people are expected to continually do more with less.

Of course, in many cases you can't conjure up more money, time or space, so you need to examine how you are using the money, time and space you already have.

Let's take some time to think about time for moment. Think about how your organisation uses time. I'll bet there are a lot of occasions when time is being wasted without people realising it's being wasted. These occasions are usually called meetings. I'm not sure if the first calendar software only allowed you to schedule meetings in 60 minute blocks, but it seems by default we have to have a meeting for an hour, when sometimes there was no need for a meeting in the first place.

And of course, if you allocate an hour for a meeting, you'll take an hour, and even then you probably won't get through what it is you need to do in that meeting, but if you say, 'Okay, you know what, you know how we normally have an hour for a meeting, we're going to give it 25 minutes', I reckon you'll get through more stuff in that 25 minutes than you would in the hour because you'll be focused. And if you do it standing up, you'll get through it even quicker.

I'm of the opinion that if you (or your people) walk out of a meeting with nothing new to think about or do, then you didn't need to be at the meeting. And if you think about how many meetings you've gone to where you've walked out and said (or, at least, thought), 'I've got no idea why I was there. What was that all about?' or 'That really could have been an email', then that's the canary struggling for breath in the coalmine. It's a sign that your organisation isn't just wasting time, but it's wasting money because you're being paid to be there. As they say, 'Time is money'. We'll be exploring how to make better use of our time in meetings in chapter 10.

When it comes to space, I'm not necessarily only considering the physical space, but of course that is useful if you're trying to do something innovative. If you're trying to use technology in a new way, it's helpful to have physical spaces that support that. But psychological space is critical. I remember working with a well-known business several years ago, and they were talking about how they wanted to embed growth mindset as part of their approach. I remember sitting with someone relatively high up the organisation chart and he said, 'You know what, I actually really do value innovation, but it's got to be right. We can't make mistakes on this'.

The tension between wanting to be innovative while remaining mistake free is problematic and it's palpable. Your people will begin to think, 'You're talking the talk, but you're not walking the walk. You're not authentic. I'm off, because that place down the road where I know they walk the walk have hit me up on LinkedIn'.

Remember it's the high performers you want to keep who end up leaving.

And when people leave there's not only the financial cost of money and time invested in that person and then, of course, the money and time required to upskill their replacement, but there's also the human cost. Morale, goodwill, group and individual mindset, and psychological safety are all affected when people leave due to frustration.

Plan: ideas and good intentions are not enough

There's a church in Sussex, England, built around the 1700s that has an inscription on one of its walls that I can only assume was sanctioned—not like the initials my kids etched in the pavement outside my house—which reads:

> A vision without a task is but a dream. A task without a vision is drudgery. A vision and a task are the hope of the world.

If we swap the word 'task' with 'plan', you can probably relate to all three sentences.

That said, in my experience I've found that the following statement is also true: 'A vision without a good plan is actually quite common'.

I'm yet to find a church with this inscription, so for now the only place you'll find it is on my whiteboard.

Even if you have the first four pillars of vision, skills, incentive and resourcing in place, without a good plan you end up with the scenario where people recognise what a great job you've done of communicating the vision. They can tell you the *what*, the *why* and the *why now*. They've got the skills to do it, and even their mate, who doesn't, knows exactly how he's going to learn to do it, and he's feeling comfortable and happy knowing he's not going to be judged for not being up to speed immediately. Everyone wants to do it, and you know what else you've given them? You've given them the time, the money and the space to do it.

How good's that?

Get your speech ready for the Boss of the Year awards ...

But woooooaaaaaahhhhh there! Hang on!

When are we starting?

Who's driving it? When are we checking in?

What's the data that we're looking for? What are we looking to learn here?

What are the milestones? Are we starting next week?

I thought we started last week!

Without a clearly communicated (there's that word again) plan, you end up with a series of false starts, people running their own race or that feeling of being in a hamster wheel, where you're working hard, you're just not sure if you're getting anywhere.

Plan to learn

There's no hard and fast rule, and you'll want to consider what planning process works best for you, but whether I'm working with individuals or teams, in the corporate, education or sporting world, the best plans we have put in place are developed using a logic model and evaluative thinking process, with regular check-ins focused on learning.

Figure 8.2 demonstrates what this might look like.

With this model, you can see how we start by considering, 'What resources are we putting into this, and what activities are we undertaking?'

This is followed by the check-in. During this check-in we share any data or outputs that we have, with a view to sharing insights and learning so as to better inform our decisions around resourcing and activities.

When our mindset is geared towards looking for learning, we ask, 'In the past 30 days, what have we learned about this?'

In the first check-in, you may find your team reporting, 'Well, we've learned that not everyone can articulate the vision' or 'We've learned that there's a bit of a skills gap there', or maybe 'You know Ali down in marketing, he doesn't seem keen. I'm not sure why yet'.

The point is that if you're embarking on something new, I'd urge you to adopt a growth mindset and say, 'Okay, well, we're changing. So clearly, we're doing something new'. It's not about whether we do it well or right, versus badly or wrong. It's about saying, especially in the early days, what do we learn from this? And then make the next iteration a little bit better.

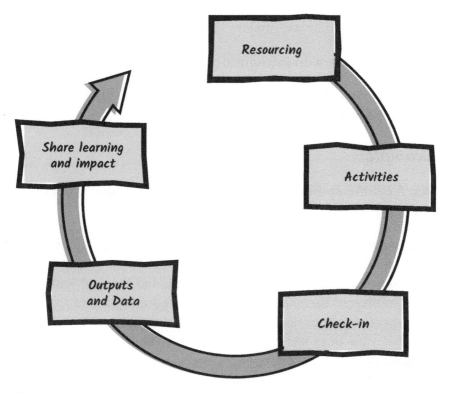

Figure 8.2: my logic and evaluative thinking model

Get this right and the change will occur. And it will stick.

How many of Knoster, Villa and Thousand's pillars of change can you tick off for a change you're currently undertaking?

The Act of Leadership: Build the bus together

Scenario 1: You've decided what change needs to occur. You create a compelling presentation and accompanying material to get people 'on the bus' and then get upset when they don't.

Scenario 2: You empower your team to build the bus they want to get on.

Lots of people can teach you how to do Scenario 1.

I'm going to share with you how to do Scenario 2.

I'll do a worked example, and then I'll ask you to consider a real-life scenario of your own.

Example:

Step 1: DEFINE in your own mind what the change is and why it needs to happen now.

Let's imagine that the change you want to make is to improve your consumer experience. This has come about because you've noticed an increase in complaints from customers, and this just happened to be at around the same time you finished a book that explored the expectations consumers now have of their trusted brands. The fact that your boss has also made it clear regularly over the past six months that they want to see an increase in customer satisfaction ratings across the whole brand adds to your resolve that something needs to happen, and the book you read has all the answers. And you have a staff meeting scheduled for Monday to talk about it.

Step 2: DISCOVER when your team or organisation is at its best with regards to this.

156

Okay, so I know that you know that customer satisfaction ratings aren't where you want them to be, but rather than verbalise that to your team—because to do that would only tell them they aren't good enough and Red mind would get all fired up—what you might say is this:

'Hey everyone, so I've just finished this really interesting book, and it's got me thinking about our consumers and how they experience our brand. The book had so many ideas and approaches that I know we're already doing, and that's what I want to hear about. I want you to go and find me examples of when we're at our best. Why do our most loyal consumers keep coming back? Over and above the financial aspect, what is it about our work that delights them?'

The idea here is to find the foundation of strength that you're going to build your change on. You're going to validate the team you have, and you're going to start from a position of positivity.

You can ask your team, 'When are you at your best with regards to consumer experience? Tell me about a time when you have been most proud of yourself and this organisation when it comes to looking after our consumers'.

You want to extract as many stories as possible. You want to hear from as many stakeholders as possible. As the leader, your voice here is the least important. Sit back and listen.

Some organisations spend a significant time on this step. Spend as long as you need.

Step 3: DREAM about what could be.

Once you've curated various examples of when your organisation is at its best, we use this to imagine new possibilities and envisage a preferred future. Having discovered 'what is best' allows people to identify their dreams for a community or organisation. They have the chance to project it into their wishes, hopes and aspirations for the future. It could be as simple as saying the following:

'Look at all this amazing stuff we have going on. Now finish this statement for me, "Wouldn't it be great if ..."'

Or you might say,

'Okay, imagine you have three wishes that if granted would fundamentally enhance the consumer experience. What would they be?'

Depending on the size of your team or organisation, you might complete this as a whole group or in smaller groups. Either way, we issue the challenge of prioritising the most important wishes or statements. We want to narrow them down to a workable number of wishes or statements. This number will vary depending on the size of your team, or the change in question.

To help prioritise they *must* fit all these criteria. If one or more of these are missing, then the wish/statement must be put aside.

Wishes/statements must be:

- *desired*—you have to really want this

- *bold and provocative*—does it stretch you in a way that attracts others?

- *affirmative*—stated as though it is happening now

- *grounded*—are there examples that demonstrate your wishes are a possibility?

- *unconditionally positive*—will it bring the best out in our people and stakeholders?

Using my example of improved consumer experience some wishes might be:

1. No consumer ever ends a call without a resolution to their issue.

2. Customer service personnel have autonomy to make decisions on the spot to resolve a consumer issue.

3. Consumers walk out of our store feeling better than when they walked in.

Step 4: DESIGN a way to address what's stopping us from already doing these things.

For each of the wish statements that have been prioritised as the ones to focus on, we explore the reasons they don't currently happen.

In the case of wish number 2, this would have all manner of financial, hierarchical and knowledge-based factors, which means it is currently not the norm for customer service personnel to operate in this manner. However, if it truly is a wish worth working for, we need to ask our people which of these factors can we influence in order for it to happen.

Again, depending on the size of your organisation you might task different groups to explore different wishes. In an ideal world, people would self-select into these groups to tackle the wishes they are most interested in.

By the end of step 4, what you have is this:

- Your people have shared with you when the organisation or team is at its best, and how they wish it could be even better with respect to the issue that's been keeping you up at night.

- Furthermore, they've identified the barriers preventing this from being the reality and remember, these are the barriers that they've said *they* can influence.

So all that's left now is for you to ask them, 'So what should we do about this?'

They want to *deliver.*

The worst-case scenario here is that they look back at you and say they don't know. At which point you can share with them some of your thoughts, or the ideas posed in the book you were reading. They are now in a position where they want to hear this.

However, the more likely and better scenario is that they come up with their own solutions, which are context-specific to your organisation, and in many cases are similar to but better than those suggested in the book as you can already see how your team have a real sense of ownership of the change.

Figure 8.3 details how this process addresses the pillars of organisational change.

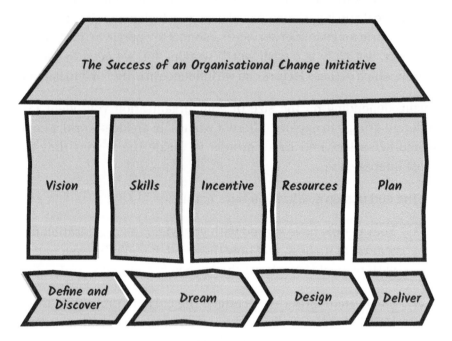

Figure 8.3: using Appreciative Inquiry to help your team build the bus

Rather than trying to convince them to buy into your vision, to get on *your* bus, you've empowered them to communicate their vision. You've watched them build the bus in front of you. And it's a fine-looking and efficient-running one!

This process is a version of an Appreciative Inquiry: A process that identifies the best in people, their organisations and the opportunities that present as a result of taking a strengths-based approach as opposed to a deficit-based approach (which tends to be more common!).

Now it's your turn.

Before you try this process out with your teams, why not use it to address the change you identified at the start of this chapter? You need to have an important rationale for doing this that might be on philosophical or operational grounds. What is that thing? Write it below, along with your reasoning for the change. (That's the *what*, *why* and the *why now*.)

....

....

....

....

When are you at your best in regard to this?

....

....

....

....

If you could have three wishes that would make this even better, what would they be? Remember they need to be desired, bold and provocative, affirmative, grounded and unconditionally positive.

Wish 1:

....

....

....

....

Wish 2:

....

....

....

....

Wish 3:

....

....

....

....

What's stopping you? What can you influence?

....

....

....

....

What are you going to do?

....

....

....

What do you notice about taking this approach?

....

....

....

....

The sweet spot

After reading this chapter:

What new insight(s) do you have?

....

....

....

....

What new intention(s) do you have?

....

....

....

....

What action(s) will you start / stop / keep doing in order to enhance your leadership?

....

....

....

....

Chapter 9

LESS IS MORE

Create space so your team can step up

This chapter in a nutshell

- you'll learn why a leader who does less, says less and knows less is just what your team needs sometimes

- you'll be encouraged to be more like a coach in your interactions with your team

- you'll learn how to stop doing everyone else's job for them

Remember Pierre from chapter 5? He was the marketing director at a large, publicly listed company with whom I was having the conversation that led me to see a huge hole in the way most organisations go about 360 feedback.

Let's hit rewind and revisit my conversation with him.

The penny drops for Pierre

[FLASHBACK]

'So what do you think?' I asked.

Pierre sat back in his chair, and tossed the paper onto the table and said, 'Yep, that's about right'.

'Really? What specifically is right about it?'

'I need to delegate better,' he said, 'That's something I've heard a lot of before.'

'So why are we still hearing it mate?'

[PREVIOUSLY UNSEEN FOOTAGE]

Pierre: 'Je ne sais pas. I guess I've just got to learn to let go of stuff.'

Me: 'What do you mean? What are you holding on to?'

Pierre: 'Pretty much everything!'

Me: 'Why?'

Pierre: 'I like to be in control, and besides I'm not entirely sure my team can do what I need them to do, to my standards.'

Me: 'Why can't you be sure?'

Pierre: 'I've never seen them do it.'

Me: 'And why's that?'

Pierre: 'Because I don't let them!'

Me: 'So, what would your day look like if you knew that your team were doing what you needed them to be doing, to a standard that was perhaps even higher than yours?'

Pierre: 'I'd have a lot more time to do the long-term strategic stuff that my boss is on my back about. That would be awesome actually, and I guess I'd have more time to really develop my team as well, which I know is important as a leader. I just don't have the time at the moment.'

Me: 'Okay, so if I'm hearing you right, you're saying that your job is actually to be across the long-term strategic stuff and to develop your team. That's what the organisation needs you to do, yes? Furthermore, is that the work you want to do?'

Pierre: 'Bien sur! Of course!'

Me: 'So, what needs to happen for that to become a reality?'

Pierre: 'I guess I need to start seeing what my team are really capable of. I need to challenge them and coach them, and I know, I know ... I need to let go.'

Me: 'Sounds like a plan. When will you start?'

Pierre: 'Don't know. I'm just so busy right now!'

[END OF FLASHBACK SEQUENCE]

The first step with Pierre was to get a perspective on not only how busy he was, but the nature of his busyness. I asked him to prepare a to-do list for the week. I asked him to include everything he felt he was *required* to do, as well as everything that he *wanted* to do. I went as far as suggesting he could also include personal tasks on here such as exercising or watching his daughter's midweek netball game.

Then, over the course of the next week, we recorded all the tasks he completed and meetings he attended. We also tracked how much time was spent on email and on the phone and the nature of those communications and we noted if and when he managed to attend netball games or get to the gym.

At the end of the week, we analysed what had accounted for his time in the previous seven days, and we compared this to his original to-do list.

If your to-do list is anything like Pierre's I'm guessing you never tick everything off, and indeed this was the case for Pierre. And again, if yours is like Pierre's, I'll bet new things keep getting added to it with monotonous regularity.

It turned out that Pierre had done everything that he felt he was *required* to do. However, he exercised only once that week, missed his daughter's netball game and had zero 1:1s with any of his team— that is, the things that he *wanted* to do.

I wanted to help Pierre realise he needn't sacrifice the things he wants to do just to complete the things he feels he has to do. I'll bet you can relate to Pierre, as it's a common challenge that leaders face.

I shared with him an age-old framework for thinking about time. Or more specifically how we choose to use our time.

During his time as President of the United States of America, Dwight D. Eisenhower was a busy guy. Among other things, he introduced the Interstate Highway System, sponsored and signed the Civil Rights Bill, brought both Alaska and Hawaii into the Union and resolved the Korean War. He did all of this while navigating the fraught relationships with the Soviet Union and ensuring the domestic budget balanced. He strikes me as someone who could use his time effectively.

In a speech in 1954, Eisenhower revealed how he viewed the decision making of leadership, saying, 'I have two kinds of problems: the urgent and the important. The urgent are not important, and the important are never urgent'.

You might be able to make an argument against Eisenhower's stance here, but for now let's play with this idea. What became known as Eisenhower's Principle suggests the following:

Important activities are those that have an outcome that enables us to achieve goals that might be professional or personal.

Urgent activities are those that demand our immediate attention, and are often more aligned with achieving someone else's goals. However, it is often these activities we concentrate on as the consequences of not dealing with them tend to be immediate.

By using a framework that Stephen Covey popularised in his book *The 7 Habits of Highly Effective People*, we assigned each of the tasks that accounted for Pierre's time into the matrix in Figure 9.1.

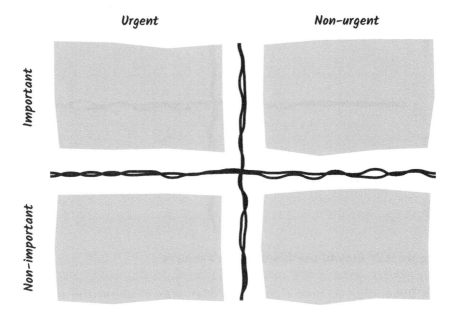

Figure 9.1: Eisenhower's matrix

What became immediately apparent to Pierre was that he was indeed busy. But much of the work that was keeping him busy was really work that others could and should have been doing. Double checking and correcting reports for the board, appeasing disgruntled clients and responding to countless emails. All of this fell into the Urgent and (seemingly) Important quadrant.

Furthermore, it became clear that most of the urgent (other people's) work *wouldn't* have fallen onto his plate had he spent more time doing the 'Important—Non-urgent' work of coaching his team and strategic planning, but, as Eisenhower implies, if the Important work lacks a deadline, then it rarely gets done because the consequences of not doing it don't seem as immediate. Unless we're deliberate about it, as Figure 9.2 shows.

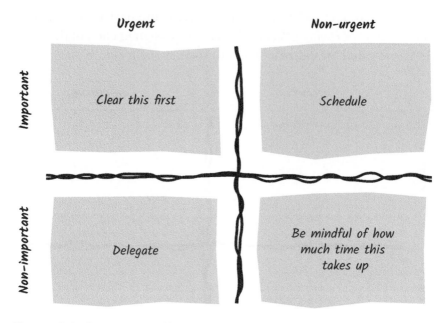

Figure 9.2: how to use Eisenhower's matrix

It's interesting to note that now Pierre was clear on the need to delegate, we could use the feedback we received in the 360 to remind him that his team wanted him to delegate. Now we had to figure out how to delegate.

Delegation isn't just giving people more work to do

Pierre is one of many leaders I've worked with who found it hard to let go of working in the way they did before becoming a leader. The temptation to keep on doing tasks is often overwhelming, especially when they appear urgent. I've lost count of the times people look at me and say, 'Yes Dan, but it's just easier if I do it myself'. That might be the case. It might be easier in the short term, but in the long term, it's detrimental, not only for yourself but the people you lead.

One of the mental challenges we have that prevents us from delegating is that many of us have had to work long and hard to reach our leadership position. We have—essentially—been rewarded for our hard work, and our input is recognised as being important for our team's success. Delegation, on the other hand, can sometimes feel like we're making ourselves less important by removing our input.

The realisation that the best leaders come to is that they're not responsible for the completion of the task; they're responsible for the people who are responsible for the completion of the task.

Leaders are responsible for creating the environment, culture and processes that lead other people to the successful completion of the task.

By using Eisenhower's matrix, Pierre was clear on what needed to be delegated, and we already knew that his team wanted to have work delegated to them, so now it was important for Pierre to consider who would be delegated what.

Running concurrently to this, you'll remember that as part of Pierre's coaching approach, we were now asking his learning team for suggestions on how he could delegate better.

For someone who had never really been able to delegate previously, this information proved really useful. As we worked our way through it, we were able to discuss what delegation really looked and felt like for the team.

His learning team gave him general advice, which you might assume was common sense (what have I told you about assumptions!), that included suggestions like:

'When you give me a task, help me understand the importance of this and how it plays into our wider strategy.'

'Can you be clear on your expectations with regards to timelines? I prefer a specific time and date rather than, "early next week".'

'Can you help me prioritise this work? Is this more/less or equally important as the project I'm currently working on?'

'If you've said you need it by Friday, can you trust me to have it ready by then? When you email me before then, it feels like you doubt me.'

'Actually, I quite like the regular check-ins as I progress through a project.'

By asking his team what suggestions they have to help him delegate, Pierre was able to do so in a fashion that was tailored to the people he led. He wasn't taking an approach from a blog post, or a book, and trying to mould his people around that. He was taking his people, and trying to mould the concept of delegation to suit them.

Perhaps the biggest stumbling block is when you believe that an individual lacks the required skillset for any of the tasks that need delegating. For those like Pierre who are reluctant to delegate in the first place, this is the point where leaders can convince themselves that only they can manage the task and it's just easier to do it themselves.

But, long term this is a misstep.

Think about it for a moment.

None of the work can be delegated to this person?

That raises the glaringly obvious question of why they are on your team.

But let's say that you're now more mindful of the tendency to not see the world exactly as it is. Let's say that now if you find yourself in this predicament, where your colleagues, team members or direct reports aren't capable of doing what's required, you'll consider that perhaps it's not a lack of capability that's causing the issue, but rather because your people aren't empowered to do the work. And as the leader, it's interesting to explore what role you're playing in this.

Allowing team members to grow with additional responsibilities displays good leadership, reflecting well on all parties. By remembering the work we did in chapter 6 to create a psychologically safe environment, we can carefully select individuals to work on projects that we know they don't have the capabilities to complete yet. However, with the right support and coaching, and development plans tailored to suit them, over time they will develop the skills necessary to become — perhaps — the go-to person down the track.

That is your job as a leader.

Delegating meant that Pierre was now doing less and this freed up more time for him to coach his team.

We'll leave Pierre there, as we delve into what I mean when I talk about coaching.

Actually, let me start by telling you what I don't mean. I don't mean that you tell people what to do or how to do it.

While that might be the domain of junior sports team coaches, it's a vastly different concept I'm talking about here.

To my mind, coaching is about saying less and knowing less.

If you have a look through the excerpts of conversations I've had with coachees you'll note two things. I tend to speak less than the coachee. And when I do speak, it's more often than not to ask a question. Go ahead. Flick back through the chapters to check. I'll wait …

See?

I'm not just being lazy in these conversations, and it's not that I don't have answers and strategies that I could offer by way of advice. It's because I'm being a coach.

The International Coaching Federation defines coaching as 'partnering with clients in a thought-provoking and creative process that inspires them to maximize their personal and professional potential'.

So, as you can see, it's open to interpretation!

For the purposes of this chapter, I'm going to dispense with the idea that you should be a coach, and rather ask you to consider how you might be *more like a coach*.

There are a couple of things that distinguish a coaching conversation from just a normal chat that you might have with a colleague or friend. The main difference is that, in a coaching conversation, you—in an attempt to be more like a coach—are deliberate in your use of a technique, or theory, that's designed to help the person you're talking to, the coachee, develop new perspectives and create a new intention or way of being, or a new way of acting with regard to an outcome that they would like to achieve.

You can be more like a coach in your formal 1:1 meetings, over a cup of coffee, or even via email or text message if you're adhering to a theory and a technique that align with coaching.

Over the past few years, I've developed a framework for coaching conversations that I've used with people from all walks of life called the SHIFT Conversation. I'll be introducing you to this in chapter 11.

However, more important than the framework is what we refer to as the way of being, or in other words, being mindful of how you 'show up' with other people.

There are three essential elements to consider if you intend to show up like a coach:

1. Be present

2. Be curious

3. Be useless.

Be present

We're deliberate in ensuring that when we're talking to somebody or when someone has approached us with something they want to talk about, we give them our full and undivided attention. We move away from our laptop, we put our phone down and we're not trying to do two things at once.

We turn our body to face them, we're very mindful of our body language and we look them in the eye. We make a commitment to that person to be entirely present for the duration of the conversation.

Be curious

I encourage leaders to be more curious than feels natural. What I mean by that is, think about the number of questions you ask or get asked during the day when one word or a short answer is enough. For example:

'How was your weekend?'

'Yeah. Pretty relaxed.'

You can tell when someone isn't really listening. They're not really interested in what's being said; they're just waiting for their turn to speak. They're waiting to tell us what they did on the weekend. They aren't genuinely curious about how we spent our weekend.

When do you find yourself not really listening, just waiting to speak?

I wonder, is it only in the office small talk that we are happy to take the first answer we hear, and then launch into our own monologue? Or might it also happen in meetings, on the phone or over email? By remembering what we learned in chapter 3 about our biases, perhaps we might be better served to remain curious a little longer than feels natural, because our natural tendencies might be leading us — and our team — astray. And this segues nicely into the third way of being ...

Be useless

When I say 'be useless', what I mean is, be deliberate in not trying to solve other people's problems. Think how many times during conversations, both at work and at home, you hear somebody throw up an issue that they're dealing with, or a challenge that they're struggling with. Because you feel that perhaps you've got some advice to give — or perhaps you have experience that would be useful to share — you're almost honour-bound to do that.

You feel compelled to. Before you even know it, you have the floor: 'Well, if you want my opinion, [INSERT ADVICE HERE]'.

Of course, you're being useful and you're offering value and you're undoubtedly helping. Except, you're probably not.

Our advice is rarely as good or as useful as we think it is. It rarely does little more than offer a short-term solution and a longer term headache.

Hint: this is one of the reasons you don't feel you can trust people with some of the work you need to trust them with!

Over the years, our desire to help others and rescue them from their struggles has seen us become their coping mechanism, and as a result—you guessed it—you end up doing their work and feeling reluctant to give them more. So the next time you feel compelled to give your advice, don't. Call to mind the need to be curious, so when you feel the urge to give advice, resist that and ask a question instead.

The Act of Leadership: Do less, say less and know less

As I mentioned, I'll introduce you to the SHIFT Conversation in chapter 11, but for now, here are some simple ways you can do less, say less and know less in a way that actually gives your team more of what they need.

Before I proceed here, I feel there should be a caveat. I was once working with a group of high-school principals, and we'd spent the morning exploring the idea of being more like a coach, and not offering advice. The group had shared many stories about how they were exhausted most of the time from rescuing situations, not only from staff but also the parent community. We were reflecting on the power of not giving advice when a phone buzzed. The principal took the phone and stepped out. We all looked around the room and gave each other knowing looks, as we knew what was happening outside. Barely five minutes after the morning session and already he was back into rescuer mode!

As he came back in, he looked around the room and said, 'Before you start, that was my deputy. There's a bloke roaming around outside the school gates with a knife'.

We all agreed there and then that there are definitely times when you should give your advice and give it quickly!

But for less pressing matters, these are some ways you might respond to someone who presents you with a challenge. This could be in a meeting, in the corridor or over email.

'Hmm, I haven't thought about that before. What do you think?'

'That's an interesting one. Let's put that out to the group to see what we come up with.'

'Imagine a mate of yours had the same drama. What would you suggest they do?'

Notice how this is a more nuanced approach than saying, 'Don't come to me with problems. Come to me with solutions'. In my experience, this albeit well-intentioned phrase usually breeds silence and damages psychological safety because it can come across as arrogant, thoughtless or intimidating.

By doing less, saying less and knowing less, what we're saying is, 'Come to me with a problem, and let's see if we can figure out a solution'.

Of course, it's a given that you're saying this in an authentic way, being entirely present. You're not trying to brush off the issue—in fact, you're willing to go deeper. At times this will feel completely counterintuitive because you may well know what they should do, and how they should do it. However, unless them not doing it your way, straight away, will result in a significant cost, why not stay curious and see how many other ways your team might be able to address the situation?

Doing this creates an environment in which your team are empowered to manage future issues themselves, and ensures they don't become dependent on you to rescue them endlessly.

At the end of the day, no matter how good your advice or idea is, it will always be your advice or your idea.

Leaders who have the biggest impact create the space and time for their people to create their own solutions.

You: 'Dan, I know all this, but I don't have time for them to figure it out on their own.'

Me: 'Fair enough, you probably don't have time right now. It is a pressing deadline, but can you recall a time when you did have time, but you chose to fill it doing something else? And what can we do to ensure you don't end up with this same situation again?'

Making time for your act of leadership

Jot down your to-do list for the next seven days.

....

....

....

....

Now allocate each of these tasks into the Eisenhower matrix in figure 9.3 (overleaf). Be sure to allocate them based on what you should be doing, not what you feel you need to do. For example, if you have a task that you know should be delegated, ensure that it is in the appropriate quadrant.

Having done that, now consider which of your team members are affected by this. Are there any who immediately jump out at you as needing your coaching around a task, behaviour or team-related matter?

Note them down below, with a statement about how you will address each one and when.

....

....

....

....

Ensure that this goes in, at the very least, your 'Important—Non-Urgent' quadrant, or perhaps even your 'Important—Urgent' quadrant.

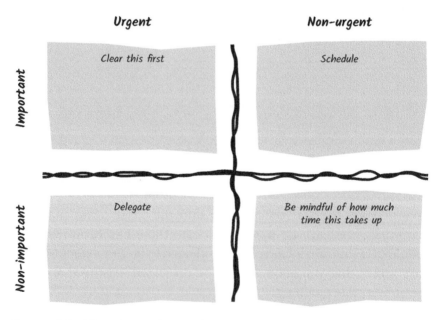

Figure 9.3: Eisenhower's matrix in action

Make a commitment to start leading your people this week by doing less, saying less and knowing less.

The sweet spot

What new insight(s) do you have?

....

....

....

....

What new intention(s) do you have?

....

....

....

What action(s) will you start / stop / keep doing in order to enhance your leadership?

....

....

....

....

Part III

THE
TACTICAL
STUFF

Part III provides advice for dealing with some of the most common challenges you might face on a day-to-day basis in your role as a leader.

Chapter 10

STOP WASTING PEOPLE'S TIME

Running meetings that matter

This chapter in a nutshell

- you'll learn to only have a meeting at the right time with the right people

- you'll see how to run effective meetings where time and money aren't wasted

- you'll see the importance of a well-crafted agenda and well-established meeting norms

To meet or not to meet? That is the question

'Honestly? I don't know.'

Jamie looked defeated. Her shoulders were slumped forward, her eyes were looking down and you could feel the energy draining from her. It was 10.30 am on a Monday. Not a great start to the week.

'What don't you know?' I asked after a moment or two of silence.

'I don't know if we achieved anything in that meeting,' she said.

I did know. They hadn't.

Except – of course – to waste everyone's time.

In the previous chapter we discussed the importance of managing your time. As a leader, it's equally, and perhaps even more, important to ensure we don't waste our colleagues' and team members' time.

In the same way in which we think of our individual time, we need to be mindful of how we prioritise our team's time.

If you're in a typical workplace, I expect that you attend or facilitate a lot of meetings through the course of a week, month or year. Are they all a worthwhile use of your time?

Do the attendees of each and every meeting leave invigorated and more engaged in their work than when they entered?

Yes? All of them? All of the time?

Fantastic. I'll see you in the next chapter. You can skip this one.

Still here?

Okay ...

Google 'meetings memes' and you'll get the gist. You're not alone. It seems that workplaces across the globe continually force people into a practice that they know isn't ideal, but for whatever reason, they continue to do so. Wasting time, and of course, wasting money.

Work out the hourly rate of the people sitting around your meeting table. It adds up pretty quickly, so it makes sense to make sure we're spending that cash wisely. Not only for the organisation's bottom line, but more importantly for those sitting around the meeting table!

I'd been working with Jamie for some time to help her become more confident in her middle leadership role. I'd offered to sit in on her meeting to get a perspective of how the group interacts. There's plenty of research that suggests just by having an observer in the room, someone from the outside, the quality of the meeting should improve. It's called 'the observer effect'. It's why you're likely to be more mindful of how you're interacting with your child or your partner if there are other people around.

But in this case, if this meeting was better because I was in the room, I was really curious to know what other meetings were like.

Where does the time go?

9.30 am: Of the 12 people invited to the 60-minute meeting, seven were present, two were, apparently, 'on their way' while no-one was sure whether or not the other three were on site that day or visiting a client.

9.37 am: Nine people are now at the table. It turns out that just one of the team is out visiting a client, and the other two texted through to say they're 'just grabbing a coffee, anyone want one?' Coffee orders are sent through.

9.43 am: Meeting starts ... or tries to. For some reason two people didn't get the agenda.

(*continued*)

9.47 am: After a quick eyeroll everyone flicks through emails on their phones to see when it was sent, and who – if anyone – was left off the email (they weren't. 'Oops sorry! I must have deleted it by mistake!'). Everyone has now had a chance to familiarise themselves with the six-item agenda.

9.56 am: I've counted five mobile phone buzzes since 9.47 am, all of which have resulted in people checking their phones.

10.01 am: They're digging into the first agenda item, but I'm beginning to notice that nobody – and I do mean nobody – ever gets to finish their sentence before someone starts talking over them.

10.04 am: Seven more phone buzzes. All but one elicits a response.

10.09 am: Two of the team are on their laptops. I don't know if they're taking notes, checking Facebook or emailing clients. What I do know is they aren't engaged in this meeting. (Hard to blame them!)

10.15 am: I've given up counting the phone buzzes. But another laptop lid has opened up.

10.25 am: Meeting wraps up. Three people didn't say a word other than 'yeah, no worries' when asked about rolling over the four agenda items they didn't get to today to the next meeting.

10.27 am: The room empties, and Jamie and I are left sitting there.

'What did you make of that?' I asked.

'Honestly? I don't know,' Jamie replied, looking defeated.

'What don't you know?' I asked after a moment or two of silence.

'I don't know if we achieved anything in that meeting,' she said.

'Well, let's look at the positives,' I said. 'You managed to get through the first two agenda items.'

'Yeah, I guess.'

That said, the first two agenda items probably shouldn't have been there in the first place. They could easily have been communicated another way, via email or a message board.

I know this fly-on-the-wall look at Jamie's meeting is an extreme example of what meetings might look like. Having observed many meetings, I know that this particular meeting is somewhat of an anomaly, but if we look closer you might see less extreme examples of what we saw in Jamie's meeting happening in yours.

Ask yourself:

- Do meetings start on time, or when everyone gets there?

- Can/should everyone speak to each agenda item?

- Do people let others finish what they're saying?

- Are people really listening or just waiting to speak?

- Do people check phones, emails or latest Groupon offers during meetings?

- Do people leave meetings with something to do as a result of being there?

- As the leader, how are you contributing to these issues?

We'll get to how the meeting should look, sound and feel shortly, but first we need to decide if we really need a meeting.

One of those memes I mentioned before, and a good rule of thumb, is:

It has to be a pretty good meeting to beat no meeting at all.

Do we need to meet?

How many times have you thought, 'Now that meeting really could have been an email'.

As a general rule, if the purpose of your meeting is simply to share information, then you might consider doing this in another way. It could be in an email, your organisational newsletter or blog, or as a short, pre-recorded video or podcast.

After 2020, when the majority of the workforce got to grips with remote working, some embraced technology and leveraged the power of asynchronous communication, meaning not everyone has to be in the same (virtual) room to hear and see the same things at the same time. Actually, we could be more targeted, and people could see and hear what they needed to at the appropriate time.

I often encourage leaders to think about the value of bringing all the people together to simply share information. (Spoiler: It's limited.)

Yet, when I mention that it could be an email or the like, I often hear, 'Yeah, but not everyone will read it. At least this way, if I know they're in the room (or on the Zoom call) I know they've heard it'.

If that really is your motivation for holding a meeting with limited value for you or your people, then I suggest creating some non-negotiable norms that ensure you aren't running your team by catering to the lowest common denominator. Continue to do this and your best people will leave. We'll explore how to set norms in more detail in chapter 12.

Other challenges present when attempting to communicate via email in that you either get the [Reply All] affliction where you receive a series of 'Got it!' and 'Thanks!' Seriously?

[Reply All] should be grounds for someone to be put on a performance management program. (I'm kidding … sorta.)

That said, you often find that much of the wisdom and knowledge in an organisation is wrapped up in email, which means when I ask my line manager something, there's a fair chance that the answer would be of use not only to me, but my colleagues. But given that I've just banned [Reply All] I'm not going to advocate for you including everyone in your email to ensure they all have the information. So what to do? Platforms like Slack or Trello allow for these types of conversations to be open, accessible and searchable by members of your organisation. Without going into it too deeply, you can set up various channels related to different aspects of your organisation, specific clients or projects. You then invite some or all of your people to join these channels, meaning that any conversation about these clients or projects, or organisational teams, are visible to all those who would benefit from them. Used well, these platforms can streamline how you communicate across your organisation, and increase the impact of the face-to-face work you do in meetings!

With all that in mind, you can use a flowchart—see figure 10.1 (overleaf)—to help you determine whether or not you need to have a meeting.

Assuming you've determined you need a meeting, let's put it together.

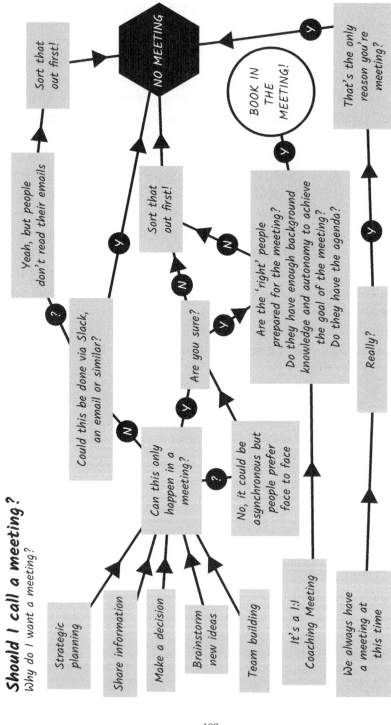

Should I call a meeting?
Why do I want a meeting?

Figure 10.1: this flowchart will help answer that question, 'To meet or not to meet? That is the question'

The Act of Leadership: Run kick-arse meetings

Say it again: 'Why are we meeting?'

Restate the purpose of your meeting to yourself just to double-check you need it. Remember, if this is a briefing to share information, it really needs to be worth pulling people away from their work. Think it through ... really ...? Okay.

The purpose of your meeting will be the guiding light as we determine who needs to be there, for how long and what work they will need to do prior to and after the meeting.

You can probably see how all these aspects would be affected by whether or not the purpose of the meeting was to make a decision or brainstorm ideas. And yet, I wonder how often we do one of two things:

1. We try to do multiple things in the same meeting.

2. We have the same people attend all meetings.

But we're going to be more deliberate from now on.

Who should be there?

Having determined the purpose, we now decide who needs to be present. As a general rule, it should be as many as is required, but no more. We're not a rock'n'roll star trying to sell out a concert. Just because we have a massive conference room, it doesn't mean we need to fill it. Our primary goal for inviting people to this meeting is to include people who will add the most value and progress us towards the goal of our meeting.

What's the goal of our meeting?

You: 'Sorry, the what?'

Me: 'The goal of our meeting.'

The goal of our meeting is the whole point of us getting together. It's what we should be able to achieve by the end of it. The goal should be clearly stated in unambiguous language so everyone who is attending the meeting knows the role they are expected to play in achieving that goal.

In other words, an agenda.

But not just any agenda.

This agenda will be read beforehand (gasp!) and will prime our attendees for action.

The agenda will be written using verbs with a strong bias towards action and outcomes. You can include as many items as you have time for.

For example:

- *The goal of our meeting* is to *decide* which CRM platform to use in the new fiscal year.

- *The goal of our meeting* is to *brainstorm* new ways to engage a younger market.

- *The goal of our meeting* is to *discuss* recent customer survey results.

- *The goal of our meeting* is to *share* our experiences of the new approach.

Only people who can contribute to the agenda and help us achieve the goal of our meeting should receive an invite. And if you're feeling really brave, you can give your people the option to decline the meeting invitation if they feel they can't contribute to the goal.

The point is, if they're in the meeting they want to contribute and we want to hear from them.

There's no simple formula for working out who should attend, but if you approach this authentically, and in the spirit we've been tapping into throughout this book, over time you'll start to feel and see the benefit of facilitating more impactful meetings.

Check in

As a general rule, I also think it's important to include five minutes at the beginning to check in with people, to ask them how they're going. This became far more pertinent in 2020, when rather than just getting straight down to business, people were asking after each other and were genuinely interested in the answers. I think we should keep this.

Questions and ponderings

I also advocate for something I used to do when I was teaching. As each lesson came to a close, I would allocate five minutes at the end for any issues, questions or ponderings that students felt were relevant but hadn't been brought up in class. I've seen a similar approach used in boardrooms, where team members are invited to contribute either verbally, or via email, in a Slack channel or similar. These musings can sometimes be addressed in the moment, or can serve as stimulus for conversation down the track, either in face-to-face meetings or discussion forums on the organisation's intranet.

Agenda

An example agenda could therefore look like this.

- *Item 1:* Check-in: 5 mins

- *Item 2:* Decide which CRM platform to use in the new fiscal year. Ensure you've read the findings in our CRM discussion group Slack channel: 15 mins maximum

- *Item 3:* Brainstorm new ways to engage a younger market: 35 mins

- *Item 4:* Questions and ponderings: 5 mins

But the agenda is only as useful as our adherence to it. And in order for us to give the agenda its best chance of succeeding I urge teams to take on the 3Ps. Team members need to be punctual, prepared and present.

Be punctual

The All Blacks Rugby Union team have a saying: 'If you're not early, you're late'.

As a leader, thinking about when you're scheduling a meeting is critical. Not only with regards to ensuring that people can turn up on time, but also turn up in the right frame of mind to contribute to the goal of the meeting. There's some research that suggests we're more creative in the morning, and more focused in the afternoon. With seven billion people or so in the world, I can't imagine this is the rule for everyone, so it could be a good idea to ask your team when works best for them.

I appreciate this level of flexibility might not be possible for everyone all the time, but I challenge you to consider when you could be more flexible for some of your people, some of the time.

For example, is the reason that Salim is now only joining meetings at the last minute (or even a couple of minutes late) because his partner works nights and as a result, Salim has to take the kids to school? Added to this, since COVID-19, he's not been able to drop them off as early as he used to. How might moving the meeting back 15 minutes allow Salim to join the meeting in a less flustered state of mind? How might that affect the meeting as a whole? How might that help build psychological safety in the team?

Be prepared

No excuses. If you're in a meeting, you need to have done the pre-work. You need to have read the report, listened to the podcast, looked through the Slack channel. You need to be prepared to share your input.

Meetings are not spectator sports, so get stuck in.

Be present

If you're in the meeting, you're in the meeting. You're not answering emails, you're not on your phone and you're not scrolling through your various social media feeds.

You're in the meeting. You're actively listening to your colleagues with the mindset of curiosity to see what you can learn in order to shape your (prepared) contribution.

You aren't multitasking, because you can't multitask.

You: 'But Dan, I can multitask.'

Me: 'No, you can't. What you're doing is doing both tasks less well than if you focused on each task individually.'

If something is more pressing (because obviously this happens at times), fine. You don't need to be in the meeting. I'll catch up with you later.

Of course, a nuanced approach is required in applying the 3Ps. For example, having a norm where there are no phones or laptops in the meeting is all well and good, until you find out that a team member's mother has just gone into hospital interstate, and she is waiting on news. In that case, of course her phone is okay in the meeting.

Of course, if 'no laptops' is a norm, that might be hard for the person who has been charged with taking the minutes of the meeting. Depending on the nature and formalities of your organisation, you might be able to ask them to jot notes on a whiteboard and a snapshot of that can suffice, until someone formalises the notes (if required) after the meeting to share with attendees and the wider organisation.

Again, there are no hard and fast rules here, but rather think about what might be possible to help more people be more present, more of the time in your meetings.

And then we get to the most important aspect of the meeting.

Create a safe psychological space

Yes, you've determined that you need a meeting. You've crafted an agenda that clearly states the goal of the meeting, and the right people are around the table—either literally or virtually—and they are punctual, prepared and ready to be present.

Congratulations, but be aware! All your hard work can be undone in an instant if you aren't mindful of the 'psychological space' that you, as the leader, create and nurture.

We've spent a lot of time in this book exploring how you as a leader show up:

- Are you Red or Blue?

- Have you left your assumptions at the door?

- Are you demonstrating a growth mindset?

- Is this a psychologically safe space?

These questions aren't only to be asked every now and then. On the contrary, I urge you to reflect on these four questions regularly. Furthermore, you could reflect on these questions before, during and after meetings.

Your efforts to improve as a leader and as a team can be quickly undone in meetings where divergent thinking or pushback are not welcome. As discussed in chapter 6, if we're not hearing different points of view and people aren't pushing back, then we should be viewing that as a canary in the coalmine that's suggesting psychological safety isn't as high as it should be. And you want it to be high, right? I mean, what level of psychological fear do you think is appropriate?

If you can actually answer that question, then put the book down and move away from the table. I can't believe you've actually got this far into the book. You're just looking for stuff to troll me about, aren't you?

However, let's say that you can't see any value in having any level of psychological fear in your team. Let's continue.

You need to ensure you are inclusive in your meetings. People are there for a reason—we made sure of that in the steps above—so if you notice they are quiet, when appropriate, draw them out with a question. Don't put them on the spot, but rather ask for their thoughts, or whether anything they're hearing is resonating with what they were thinking about in the lead-up to the meeting. Or perhaps a more dominant voice is getting a little too much airtime. Rather than saying you've heard enough from them, you can gently direct them to do something specific like, 'Thanks Dan, great input. I'm wondering for the next few minutes, could you just sit back and listen for the common themes that come out in conversation? Could you jot them down, and we'll revisit them before we move on?' Make sure this isn't busy work, but rather another form of data gathering that you can use to evaluate the effectiveness of the meeting.

How effective are our meetings?

Being able to evaluate the effectiveness of a meeting is super important, but you're not always the one best placed to do that.

How many times in the past 12 months have you been asked your opinion on how effective a meeting was? How many times were you asked for your ideas as to how the organisation might improve meetings?

Let's flip that. How many times have you asked these questions of your people? How many times have you sought their feedback on how the meetings you manage are going?

I'm not saying you should do this all the time, but perhaps some of the time might be useful. And at least once. Now. As a result of reading this book, perhaps you might go and find out from your people what they think about how meetings run in your organisation.

You could use this chapter as stimulus, or you could ask your team some simple yes/no questions, with space for them to elaborate on why they feel that way. Feel free to come up with your own questions. These are just to get you started:

- Do our meetings lead to a stronger team or organisation?

- Do our meetings empower you to do your job better?

- Do you ever feel you're in meetings that you don't need to attend?

- How clear are agendas and goals for the meetings we have?

- Do you feel heard in our meetings?

- Do we have too many meetings?

- How does the timing of our meetings suit you?

- Are our meetings regular enough?

- Do your colleagues contribute well to our meetings?

- Are our meetings professional and respectful?

The sweet spot

After reading this chapter:

What new insight(s) do you have?

....

....

....

....

What new intention(s) do you have?

....

....

....

....

What action(s) will you start / stop / keep doing in order to enhance your leadership?

....

....

....

....

Chapter 11

NO MORE SH!T SANDWICHES

Have better 1:1s with your team

This chapter in a nutshell

- you'll learn why traditional approaches to workplace feedback don't work

- you'll learn my framework for a SHIFT Conversation

- you'll be encouraged to consider who would benefit from a SHIFT Conversation immediately

Think back to chapter 5 where we discussed some of the tripwires that trigger Red mind when we receive feedback.

- *Tripwire #1:* We don't believe it — 'They're wrong!'

- *Tripwire #2:* It depends who it's from — 'Who are they to tell me that?'

- *Tripwire #3:* It's personal — 'Maybe they're right. Maybe I'm an impostor.'

Being aware of these tripwires means we can now take a more nuanced approach to how we give feedback. And by more nuanced, I mean let's get rid of the sh!t sandwich. You know what I mean: negative feedback sandwiched neatly between two positive points.

Your direct report comes into their performance review hoping for some positive feedback because they feel they work hard for the organisation and it would mean a lot to them for that to be acknowledged and to be told they are a valued member of the team.

You may have been on a training program or read a book or blog post that told you, when giving feedback, start with a positive. So, you start with a positive. Then you guide the session to a point where you can offer some constructive criticism before finishing, with a flourish, with some more positive affirmations about your direct report.

Et voilà, a sh!t sandwich

The facilitator of that training program would be proud, and rather than reading a book about giving feedback, you're now thinking you should *write* one given how well you prepared and delivered that sandwich.

If only this type of feedback actually worked. But of course, it doesn't.

You know that, because it's never really worked for you, has it?

Yet when we become leaders we think that somehow, this time, things will be different. We think that the sandwiches we prepare will be better digested.

But they aren't.

There are many reasons why this feedback doesn't work, not least the tripwires outlined at the start of the chapter, but one reason is that, if as a leader you feel compelled to use the sh!t sandwich as a way to address poor performance, there's every chance you'll dilute your feedback to the point where the person you're talking to doesn't recognise its importance, and as a result you'll see no shift in behaviour.

If, on the other hand, there isn't an issue with poor performance, and you're using the sandwich to encourage growth or the setting of stretch goals, then could I suggest to you a better alternative?

> **You:** 'Woah, I need to know how to kick people up the arse over poor performance or behaviour!'

> **Me:** 'Patience, young grasshopper. We'll dig into that in chapter 12. For now, let me show you one way to help people be their best. Doing this more often will mean you have to kick arse less often.'

In chapter 9, I spoke about being more like a coach. Feedback sessions intended to inspire growth are the perfect time to practise being more like a coach, and in keeping with the idea of being present, curious and useless you might wish to deploy the SHIFT Conversation.

The Act of Leadership: Have a SHIFT Conversation

Over the past few years, I've developed the SHIFT Conversation to help facilitate coaching conversations between myself and clients, and also for leaders to use with and among their teams.

Coaching is facilitated through conversations that assume the coachee (the person being coached) is the person best positioned to identify and act upon issues within their context. In my experience, most people can work out what they need to work on, and if we give them the time and space to come up with it themselves, they are far more likely to follow through with it.

Coaching respects and encourages autonomy, while focusing on the mastery and purpose. The nature of the coaching conversation—when done well—also increases psychological safety and a sense of belonging. If you want to increase engagement, performance, wellbeing and team dynamics it's a no-brainer.

Broadly speaking, SHIFT stands for Scan, Hurdle, Incentive, Focus, Tactics, and I've developed SHIFT as a way to map a conversation. It's not a script that needs to be followed lock-step; rather, it's a way for you to locate where you're at in a conversation and where you might go next.

I'm going to walk you through what a typical SHIFT Conversation might sound like when you're having a 1:1 conversation with one of your team members.

For the moment, we're going to assume that this is not a 'difficult' conversation (we'll tackle those in the next chapter).

Let's assume here that you, as the leader, are seeking to understand a little bit more about your team member so you can help them be the best version of themselves that they can be.

Scan

The SHIFT Conversation starts off with the **Scan**, in which you're trying to get the lay of the land. You're trying to figure out what's happening, what's going on.

'How's your week been?'

'What's on your plate right now?'

'What does your to-do list look like?'

'What projects are you working on?'

The scan also offers an opportunity for the person you're working with (the coachee) to settle into the conversation, as it's not unusual to hear, or see, a sense of fatigue, a deep breath out as they transition from the busyness of their day or their role into the coaching space. It's in this space where the coachee can step back from being 'on' and is given the time to focus on themselves and check in with how they're going. It's a real change of pace for many people and as the coach you can facilitate this with a good scan.

For this to be worthwhile, it has to be relaxed to enable the coachee to think more broadly. The gist of the scan is that you're trying to see what's on their plate and this might venture into home life, or the coachee might talk about issues that are of a personal nature, which in one way or another affects how they show up and their effectiveness at work.

As a leader, you can't be afraid to go there.

You're not their psychologist, therapist, priest or parent, so you're not expected to counsel them, but it is worthwhile if the coachee goes there, to go with them. Nothing says, 'I'm not interested' or 'You're not part of this tribe' more than a leader or a boss who thinks you can just leave your personal life at the door. That may be old-school thinking and it may have worked in the past (I doubt that it worked in the past), but nowadays the most progressive and authentic leaders I know are well aware that we're whole beings. We're a blended mix of our personal and professional selves when we're at work and at home, perhaps even more so since 2020 as the boundaries between work and home have become increasingly blurred.

In my experience, it will depend on the nature of your relationship with the coachee as to the length of time that you spend in the scan, but when you feel you've got a fair picture of what's going on, you then want to segue into the second element. And one way I typically segue into that second element is along the lines of:

'Wow, it sounds like there's a lot going on. You've got a lot on your plate. So tell me, what's the biggest challenge that you face right now?'

And it's that question which moves us from the scan into what I call the **Hurdle** phase of the conversation: 'What's the biggest challenge you face right now?'

Hurdle

It's quite common for people to perceive the word hurdle, or 'challenge', as a negative, but I'm more deliberate about framing the question neutrally.

When I'm working with an athlete who, for example, needs to jump over hurdles in order to win a medal, then those hurdles can't be seen as negatives — those hurdles must be seen as part and parcel of their success. They have to be seen as the pathway to their success. You can't be an Olympic hurdler if you don't like hurdles.

The same goes for the word 'challenge'. Being able to frame challenges in the positive as well as the negative gives you a real broad spectrum and a wider scope to help and support your people as best you can when we're not just focusing on problems.

All that said, because it's quite common for people to perceive these things as negative, that might be the first thing that comes up. Something they're struggling with.

But what's interesting to note is that, in my experience, when you ask somebody what their biggest challenge is, they very rarely tell you. Very rarely are they able to drill down into specifically what the challenge is. Rather, they'll talk about the challenge that's perhaps most pressing or most urgent, or perhaps it's the one that they think is easiest to talk about.

A common example of this is:

Me: 'What's the biggest challenge you face right now?'

Coachee: 'Oh, I'm just so busy. There's not enough hours in the day!'

And that might feel very real to them; of course it does. Very few people actually feel that they have enough time to do everything they want. We've spoken about this already in the book. And because so many people can resonate with this, often, it's a good way not to talk about your specific challenge.

When somebody says, 'Oh, I'm just so busy', you'll often hear someone else say, 'Oh, tell me about it. I'm so busy too. How fast has this year gone? I just don't have time to do all the things I need to do'. In the blink of an eye, we're no longer talking about that person's specific challenge because someone was just waiting for their turn to speak.

This is what I say:

Me: 'What's the biggest challenge you face right now?'

Coachee: 'Oh, I'm just so busy. I just don't have enough time.'

Me: 'What is it that you're not able to do that if you had more time you would be doing?'

Now we're into it. And you'll notice that I *didn't* advise them to use Eisenhower's matrix at the first suggestion that time was their issue. Remember, stay present, curious and useless.

At first, you'll find this hard, and the coachee won't be used to it because, a lot of the time, we only speak superficially about challenges. Many of us don't go into much depth about our stuff because for a lot of people it's not comfortable, and it's not something we're used to doing. That's why at dinner parties, everyone sort of nods knowingly when people talk about their boss or about not enough time or about the kids. Everyone has a knowing nod, but rarely do people really go much deeper than that and tackle the real issues.

But in a SHIFT Conversation, we need to go deeper in order for it to be a useful conversation.

Me: 'What's the biggest challenge you face right now?'

Coachee: 'Oh, I'm just so busy. I just don't have enough time.'

Me: 'What is it that you're not able to do that if you had more time you would be doing?'

Coachee: 'Well, I don't know, all the things I need to do.'

Me: 'Okay, so let's list some of those things. What are the things that you need to do?'

…

Together we complete the list.

…

Me: 'There's a lot there that you need to do. What are some of the things that you *want* to do, which you currently can't because of a lack of time?'

This is when it can get quite interesting. I've had people come up with:

Coachee: 'Well, I'd just love to be able to get home and read a story to my daughter before she goes to bed and go and see my son play soccer on a weekend.'

But, as the coach, I'm still not done.

Me: 'Okay, so what's the challenge for you when you can't do those things? Why is that an issue for you?'

In my experience, and it doesn't matter whether I'm working with corporate executives, athletes or educators, this is the point in the conversation when people suddenly realise this is not the normal type of conversation they're used to. It's at this point when they think 'Okay, this is interesting now, because I'm saying things out loud that I probably haven't said before'.

And if you remain present, curious and useless a fraction longer you hear that the real challenge is:

'I'm really concerned that the relationship with my daughter is fracturing.'

'My son genuinely believes I care more about my work than I do about him.'

These are real challenges for people. These are deep challenges for people, and if we try to tell ourselves these challenges aren't affecting us in the workplace, then we're kidding ourselves.

Now, of course, it's equally likely that the real challenge might remain located in the workplace and that might sound more like:

'I don't feel I'm getting the best out of my team, and in my last role I prided myself on being able to do that.'

'I don't know how I'm going to talk to the group next week. I feel like a fraud.'

We can't get clear of a hurdle until we're clear on what and where the hurdle actually is, and while there is no hard and fast rule as to when you've done that, you will sense the mood changes in the conversation, and you'll know you've hit upon a real challenge or at least come close to the real challenge. It's important to recognise here that regardless of whether it's a personal challenge or a professional one, the impact is likely to be felt in the workplace and at home so it's important at this point to reflect back on what we've heard so far.

Me: 'Okay, so if I've heard you right, it sounds like your challenge is you're not spending enough time with your daughter and you feel like that's really affecting your relationship. And this is affecting how you show up at work. You're starting to resent the work that you have to do, and because you're resenting the work, perhaps the level of output, or perhaps your effectiveness in your role, perhaps that's starting to weigh in as well. Is that right?'

With that question, 'Is that right?', you're giving the coachee the opportunity to either confirm or clarify. 'Yep. That's absolutely right. I've never said it out loud before, but that's exactly how I'm feeling', or 'I'm not quite sure if that's what I meant. I think you've put words in my mouth there. I think what I really mean is ...'

By giving them the chance to confirm or clarify, you help them get to the point. You help them to articulate what it is that's causing them a real headache. What's the real challenge? And that's when we want to segue into the third element of the SHIFT Conversation, the **Incentive**.

Incentive

Once the coachee has confirmed or clarified their hurdle or challenge, we repeat it out loud, or sometimes I even write it down with great ceremony.

And then I ask:

> **Me:** 'So with regards to that, what do you want, what do you want to come of it?'

And it doesn't matter who I ask, when I ask—whether it's to an individual or a group—it always plays out like this:

> **Me:** 'So with regards to that, what do you want? What do you want to come of it?'

> **Coachee:** 'I don't want to keep arguing with my daughter. I don't want to have to work so late!'

What do you notice about the coachee's response?

Almost without exception over the past few years whenever I've asked people what they want they tell me all the things they *don't* want.

Or they tell me things they want other people to do.

> **Me:** 'So with regards to that, what do you want, what do you want to come out of it?'

> **Coachee:** 'I *want my boss* to realise I've got a life outside of this place!'

While it's perfectly natural for us to talk about things that we don't want, or things we want others to do, it's not helpful. In fact, it's quite disempowering. It puts us in a position where we don't have much control over our destiny. We cede autonomy and our sense of volition to others, or to the situation that we're faced with.

In this case, I find it useful to reflect back what I've heard. I'm not telling people that they're wrong or that they shouldn't want others to understand them. But what I do want to do is reflect back on what I've heard and then gently challenge them to rephrase what they've said in the affirmative and in a way over which they have at least some control.

For example, 'I don't want to keep arguing with my daughter' becomes 'I want to get on better with my daughter'. Or 'I want my boss to realise I've got a life outside of this place!' becomes, 'I want clearer boundaries between work and home'.

Now, rather than focusing on what we don't want or what we want others to do, we're just making a statement that says, 'Okay, I want this'. And it's stated in the affirmative and if you achieve it, it would be a positive. And, while we still need to have other parties buy into it on some level, it is now stated in a way in which the coachee has—at least some—control.

Once we have that, we write it down or we make a point of reiterating it.

Then we can move into the **Focus** part of the conversation.

Focus

Now, at this point, I'd like to point out that the SHIFT conversation without the F, isn't a very good conversation.

This is a critical moment because now we focus in on what it is that the coachee can do with regard to achieving what they want. Again, I want to reiterate the importance of staying present, curious and above all, *useless*, at this point. Yes, I'm sure you have a great book recommendation for parents who want to improve their relationship with their kids. I'm sure you've read a great blog post on putting in boundaries between work and home, but now is not the time to share these. We're going to hold all of that back, because what we want to ask here is:

> **Me:** 'Okay, well, what could you do? What might you do that could help you get what you want?'

I often give a time limit and say, 'All right, well, let's see how many ideas we can come up with in five minutes'.

People often think, 'Are you kidding me? I've struggled with this for ages, and you're only giving me five minutes!'

The reality is you actually don't need to think that quickly to come up with lots of ideas in five minutes because we're not putting any criteria on the quality of these ideas. We just want to get a flow of thinking happening. As the coach, your only role at this point is to lay down the challenge along the lines of:

'All right, come up with 20 ideas in five minutes. So what could you do?' And then you just write them down as they come out. You don't offer any judgement. You don't say, 'Whoa, I wouldn't do that mate', and, as counterintuitive as it sounds, try not to say things like, 'Oh, that's a great idea'. What happens when we say 'that's a great idea' is often it's not a great idea, it's just the best idea we've heard so far, and we gravitate to that at the expense of all the other ideas that might have come out afterwards but don't. Let the ideas flow without any qualification. You're just going to be writing them down, saying, 'Okay, what else could you do?'

Sometimes people will self-censor their ideas because they're worried that their ideas aren't good enough. In that case, come back with, 'Well, that's fine. Let's start with a bad idea. Let's start off with a crazy idea'. The role of the coach at this point is to keep the flow of thinking going.

When the coachee has come up with as many ideas as they can— and by the way, if you've set a five-minute time limit, and the flow of ideas shows no sign of abating as you clock up 300 seconds, stay there, keep mining those ideas until you feel that the well has run dry—it's time to close out the conversation. It's time to use **Tactics**.

Tactics

> **Me:** 'Okay, so of all these ideas, what will you do? And when will you do it?'

The 'best' ideas on the list are ones that the coachee will actually act on, ideally in the next 24–48 hours.

A great idea is not a great idea if it only stays on the paper or in your head.

The coachee commits to an idea. They write it down and then you ask a really important question, which sounds like this:

'Okay, so you've said you're going to block out time in your diary this week for taking your daughter for a bike ride. You're putting that in the diary? Okay. When should I check in with you to see how you went with that?'

Did you hear that? 'When should I check in with you?'

Note the language that I've used there: 'check in' (this is not 'check up'). This is not a compliance issue. This is not a performance management conversation. This is you as a leader, or as a coach, helping the coachee get to a place where they have a new insight, where they're feeling better about things and where they'll be able to perform better, both at home and at work.

When they suggest the time to check in, make sure that you do. It could be a text message or an email, or if you work nearby, swing by the office and have a chat. It could be over coffee, or part of your next 1:1 chat depending on when that's scheduled for. The point is, if you've said you're going to check in and they've asked you to check in, then make sure that you check in.

And the final question that helps you and the coachee see the value of the conversation is to ask: 'What did you find useful about that?'

This is important because it validates the coaching process for both you and the coachee. You'll notice that you still haven't recommended the book or blog post. And in all likelihood you won't need to because the coachee has actually committed to doing something as opposed to being given a book they won't read.

Why SHIFT?

SHIFT differs from other frameworks (SMART, GROWTH etc.) in that these frameworks assume the coachee already has a goal. SHIFT allows the coachee to explore many aspects of their context before establishing their goal. You should also bear in mind that the SHIFT can happen in five minutes or over the course of many conversations.

It's not uncommon for a conversation to actually take the form of SHISHIHIFIFT, meaning that you may well return to various elements before moving on. As I said before, it's not a script, but rather a way for you to be able to locate yourself in the conversation and give yourself a sense of where you could take the conversation next. If you remember the distinction between a coaching conversation and a chat, it's the deliberate use of a technique or theory designed to help the coachee develop new perspectives and create a new intention, a new way of being or a new way of acting with regard to an outcome that they would like to achieve.

Even though I've given examples of the language I would use in a SHIFT Conversation, it's important for you to be comfortable with the words coming out of your mouth. How might you maintain a sense of curiosity in your questioning throughout a SHIFT Conversation?

Example scan questions

- What's been happening?

- What else?

- Where do you see yourself in six months?

- Where would you like to see yourself in six months?

- What's your current situation?

- What's on the horizon?

- Where are you now and where would you like to get to?

- How would you like to grow over the next 12 months?

Come up with three of your own:

....

....

....

Example hurdle questions

- What's holding you back?

- What's the real challenge?

- What hinders you?

- What needs to change? What's stopping you?

- What's the biggest challenge for you right now?

- Why haven't you already?

- What's a positive challenge you have right now?

- If we could remove one obstacle, what would it be?

- What's the most exciting challenge you're faced with?

- What have been the big issues in the past?

- What's getting in the way of you thriving right now?

Come up with three of your own:

....

....

....

Example incentive questions

- On a scale of 1–10, how important is this to you?

- To what extent are your motivators extrinsic?

- What's in it for you?

- What do you want?

- If money and time was no object, what would you like to do about this?

- What are your intrinsic motivators?

- What will achieving this mean to you?

- Why's that important to you?

- How have you felt in the past towards something like this?

Come up with three of your own:

....

....

....

Example focus questions

- What could you commit to doing?

- What first steps could you take?

- What does that encourage you to do?

- What might you do in the next seven days?

- Is there anything that jumps out at you as being something you can tackle immediately?

Come up with three of your own:

....

....

....

Example tactics questions

- How will you do this?

- What help do you need?

- Do you have the time to commit to this?

- Do you feel you have the skills/ability to do this?

- If we were mapping this out on a piece of paper, how many steps would be involved?

- On a scale of 1–10, how confident are you that you can achieve this in the set time?

- Who will you enlist in your efforts?

- When are we checking in again?

- What was most useful here?

Come up with three of your own:

....

....

....

Who can you think of who would benefit from a SHIFT Conversation?

....

....

....

....

The sweet spot

After reading this chapter:

What new insight(s) do you have?

....

....

....

....

What new intention(s) do you have?

....

....

....

....

What action(s) will you start / stop / keep doing in order to enhance your leadership?

....

....

....

....

Chapter 12

HAVE LESS DIFFICULT CONVERSATIONS

Start having adult ones instead

This chapter in a nutshell

- you'll be encouraged to reflect on your mindset leading into 'difficult' conversations, and whether or not that's helpful

- you'll be introduced to two techniques to enhance clarity and accountability in your team

- you'll be challenged to stop thinking of these conversations as 'difficult'

Why most people find difficult conversations ... well ... difficult

'Why don't you just talk to them about it? What's the real challenge for you here?' I asked.

Sohail had spent the last 10 or 15 minutes explaining to me his biggest challenges with some of his team members. But that's when the penny dropped for him.

He'd been in his middle management position for over a year when I met him, and my meeting with him was something of an ad-hoc arrangement.

I'd met with his general manager, Jenny, for coffee just for a bit of a catch-up and to bounce some ideas around, and in passing she mentioned she was wondering if I might have a chat with Sohail to see how he was going. The organisation had recognised him as someone of high potential, but of late his line manager was becoming concerned that he hadn't adapted to his new role as team leader, particularly with regard to his ability to hold people to account. Jenny suspected his team was starting to fracture and wanted to get an outside perspective.

A week or so later I was sitting in the same coffee shop, this time with Sohail. We'd chatted a bit over email, and he knew I was a coach and that Jenny was keen for us to chat in order to help Sohail further develop his leadership, something that Sohail was very keen to do.

As we settled in, I asked him the 'scan' question that I use when I'm meeting someone for the first time, 'So mate, tell me a little bit about your role'.

'Oh you know, pretty standard. I'm in charge of the sales team, so everything that goes with that really', came the typically superficial response we give when someone asks us what we do for a living. But you know courtesy of the last chapter that I wouldn't be happy with that, so I asked follow-up questions for another 10 minutes to get more clarity around his day-to-day operations.

'What does a typical day look like?' 'How many people are on your team?' 'What's the most enjoyable aspect of your role?' 'What's the most challenging?' (See what I did there?)

Up until I asked him what was most challenging about his role, he appeared to be – in his words – 'All good. No problems'.

But having asked him what was most challenging about his role, I listened as Sohail embarked on a monologue around the various characters in his team who he thought were undermining him as a leader, going around him to senior management to raise issues, or weren't following through on project assignments and of course there were the ones who were always late to, or disengaged in, team meetings.

Sohail told me how he didn't want to go 'higher up' with his concerns as he felt that would tarnish his reputation and prospects for advancing his career, so he was busy covering up for the rest of his team. He was starting to resent some of the characters in his team, even though he told me they're 'Good people, they just don't care as much about the team and the work as I do.'

'Have you spoken to them about this?' I asked.

'Not yet. I'm hoping I won't have to. They're professionals. Surely they know they need to lift their game.'

'Why don't you just talk to them about it? What's the real challenge for you here?' I asked.

[Momentary silence as the penny drops]

'I don't really know how to say what I need to say. Besides, I don't like confrontation, and I don't want to risk the relationship. I mean it's not every day. Most of the time they're fine.'

If I had a dollar for every time I'd heard someone tell me they avoid having conversations because they don't like confrontation I reckon I'd easily break $100.

By aiming to avoid difficult conversations, you end up having to have more.

The irony is that by seeking to avoid confrontation in the moment, leaders end up with more confrontation down the track.

But what if 'difficult' conversations needn't be difficult at all?

What if just by calling them 'difficult' conversations we're setting ourselves up for failure or—at best—a lot of angst? In fact, what if we've been setting ourselves up for failure from the beginning?

Most issues that lead to 'difficult' conversations stem from one or more people not acting in a way that's in accordance with the leader's expectations, those of the rest of the team or those of the wider organisation, and *herein* lies the issue.

We assume (there's that word again) that everyone knows what these expectations are, and we then—in our mind at least—hold people to account to these expectations, getting annoyed when they don't meet the standards. We might get upset by what a person does or doesn't do or the manner in which they do or don't do it. Someone may indeed do everything that's required, but the manner in which they go about their work, to your way of thinking, isn't professional.

You assume they know their behaviour isn't professional, and next time you're sure, or at least hopeful, they'll address it. Until next time comes around and it's clear they're carrying on as before.

We think people are on the same page when in reality some of us aren't even in the same library.

We think that if we say, 'We need to be professional', then people will all agree. And in most organisations they do agree, of course. What they don't agree on is what 'professional' actually means.

When we've finished outlining how the project will roll out and we ask, 'Does anyone have any questions?' we view the fact nobody raises their hand as a sign that everyone understands what's expected of them. In reality there are many reasons that hands don't go up, ranging from a lack of psychological safety to the fact that it's 7.30 pm and people just want to get home.

When we ask, 'Are we all on the same page?' replies of, 'Yeah, more or less' or 'Yeah, pretty much' should not be taken as an indication of a job well done—it should be taken as a sign that people are not 100 per cent aligned.

> **You:** 'Come on Dan, near enough is good enough, isn't it? They're all educated professional adults. Surely I don't need to spell it out?'
>
> **Me:** 'Yes you do. S P E L L I T O U T.'

The reason you need to spell it out is because you can only (really) hold people accountable for what they said they'll do, in the manner in which they said they'll do it, against agreed norms. Yes, I know they have their job descriptions, and they should all know what to do and how to do it, but how's that working out for you? Figure 12.1 shows what happens over time if we don't start on the same page.

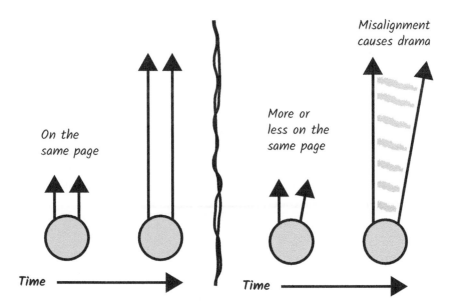

Figure 12.1: we drift apart over time

So, how do we go about setting agreed norms?

Here's a strategy we've used with professional sporting teams, corporate teams and school leadership groups. It focuses on *how* we do our work as a team. And it works like this.

The leader sets the scene at an appropriate time. Obvious milestones like the start of a new calendar year or financial year are good times to do this, but I also encourage leaders to consider using the start of a new project or the addition of a new member of the team as opportunities to engage in this kind of work. For a football team it could be in the pre-season.

If none of those present for you in the short term, and you'd like to address norms with your team, then you could use finishing this book as the stimulus. You might say something like:

'So, I've just finished reading this book on leadership (in fact, I have to go online and rate it five stars and leave a glowing review) and it's got me thinking. I suspect that while we're more or less on the same page in terms of our expectations for this team, we may not be 100 per cent the same. Can we have a chat about that?'

As the discussions unfold, you might start noting down some common themes where people aren't quite aligned. It might be around expectations of sharing information, or the time it takes to respond to email. It might be that some people turn up unprepared for meetings, or submit sloppy work for others to correct. The important thing here is to ensure we talk about issues, not people.

From here, you can identify specific issues for a deeper discussion in order to set the new expectations moving forward.

Jot down some of the expectations you have for your own team that some people aren't living up to.

....

....

....

....

The next move is to put the specific issues to your team by asking, 'Is this acceptable?'

To illustrate, I'm going to use expectations around meetings. Imagine we've had a bit of a chat about things, and then I ask:

'So we've had a good chat here, and we've heard some common issues that people have brought up. So moving forward, on this team, is it acceptable for people to be on their phones during meetings?'

My team and I have done this where people stand on different sides of the room. The left-hand side for 'acceptable' and the right-hand side for 'unacceptable'.

For the vast majority of the issues you bring up, you will have a clear majority, if not the entire group, standing on one side. In that case, as the leader you can create the norms to fit the people you have, but of course sometimes people will not be able to choose, and they'll be meandering around the middle of the room, which is the spot I call: 'unacceptable, but understandable'.

In the case of using phones in meetings, if your people gravitate to 'unacceptable but understandable', meaning they know it's unacceptable to have phones in meetings but occasionally it will be understandable, you as the leader say this:

'Right, I don't want to be continually on your back about when or why phones are being used in meetings. Can you discuss this as a group and come back to me with how we're going to handle it?'

Let *them* create the norm. How are they—as educated professional adults—going to manage that?

Ditto for questions like:

'Is it acceptable for people to be late to meetings?'

'Is it acceptable for people not to have read the agenda before meetings?'

'Is it acceptable for people to cut a colleague off in meetings?'

Is it acceptable, unacceptable, or unacceptable but understandable?

Once you have your defined list of behaviours, you then go around the room one by one asking if people can commit to these. Of course you can review after two or three months, but for now, can they commit? So now we are all on the same page. In some organisations they actually all sign the same page with these new behaviours listed. If anyone hesitates to commit, that's a sign that you need to dig deeper into the issue to figure out what the barrier is for that person. Take as much time as you need for this.

You: 'But Dan, I don't have time for this.'

Me: 'You can make time for this now, or make sure you have a lot of time to sort out all the dramas later.'

It was this process that helped us create the 3Ps of meetings that I mentioned in chapter 10. The team we worked with know exactly what's expected of them and each other when they talk about being punctual, prepared and present.

As a result, having conversations around this is less difficult. Especially when you incorporate the thinking of Jonathan Raymond, who created the Accountability Dial™ to help leaders hold their people accountable without resorting to blame, judgement or shame.

In his book *Good Authority*, Raymond presents us with this simple yet incredibly powerful tool that, when used in conjunction with the norm-setting activity above and the SHIFT Conversation, gives you a suite of options when you're faced with a conversation you know you need to have but are hoping not to.

I was so impressed with the Accountability Dial and how readily people could get their heads around it, I invited Jonathan on to my *Habits of Leadership* podcast in 2020 to discuss it in more depth. He told me the purpose of the dial is to say, 'Okay, where am I in this conversation? Am I at a step 1, a step 2 a step 3, a step 4 or a step 5?'

His book offers some excellent scripting for the kinds of things you might say and when you might say them for each point of the dial, but in essence the dial is to help you understand how much urgency, how much authority, how much fire you are bringing into that conversation. Raymond told me this is his primary determining factor of whether or not a person is going to listen to you. 'Because if you bring too much fire relative to the moment, I'm going to tune you out, I'm going to get defensive. If you bring not enough fire, not enough urgency, not enough authority, I'm going to assume it's not that big a deal. And tuning the instrument of people management, that's what the Accountability Dial's for.'

The other main issue that the dial addresses is the timing of when a leader speaks to a person. Too often we don't act early enough, and the behaviour gradually gets worse until we finally do bring it up, and we usually bring it up too late in the piece. Figure 12.2 (overleaf) is my version incorporating my SHIFT conversation.

Remember, you can only (really) hold people accountable for what they said they'll do, in the manner in which they said they'll do it, against agreed norms. In our illustration, those agreed norms are to be punctual, prepared and present for meetings.

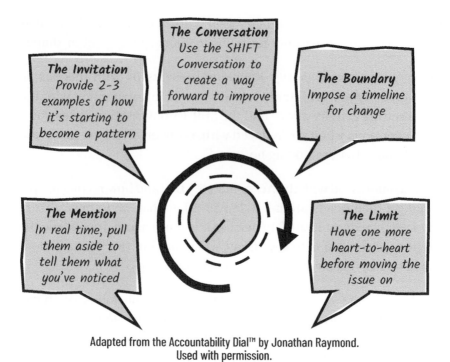

Adapted from the Accountability Dial™ by Jonathan Raymond.
Used with permission.

Figure 12.2: my version of Raymond's Accountability Dial

The Act of Leadership:
Hold people accountable

Imagine for a moment that your direct report, Darren, turned up for a meeting and it was apparent pretty quickly that he hadn't prepared. He hadn't read the agenda, and wasn't able to contribute as well as he might have to your 'goal of the meeting'. Of course, you weren't the only one to notice, and even if your team aren't talking about it, they're definitely thinking about it.

In the past you might have let this slide, thinking it's a one-off—besides you don't want to damage the relationship, and you're not keen on confrontation.

But now, armed with the new norms that Darren put his name to and the Accountability Dial, you feel more comfortable addressing

Darren's lack of preparedness by deploying what Raymond calls 'The mention'.

Step 1: The mention

The mention happens in real time, in private, and sounds like this:

'Hey Darren, I noticed that you hadn't read the agenda for today. Is everything all right?'

That's it.

Notice the language I've used. It's neutral and is devoid of blame, judgement or shame. I'm saying I noticed something, and I'm wondering if everything's all right.

After hearing me mention it, Darren is likely to go one of two ways.

Either he says something like, 'Yeah, sorry I'm flat out at the minute. It won't happen again'. Or things might not be all right. He might have an issue at home he's dealing with and he's struggling to keep on top of things. As the leader you might be able to assist in supporting Darren through the tricky time.

Either way, the mention avoids confrontation or conflict, and by virtue of asking, 'Is everything all right?' it serves to build the relationship. It doesn't damage it.

At 'Utopia Inc.' the mention was all that was required and from that day on Darren always read his agenda.

In the real world, however, it might take more than one mention.

If, when you initially mentioned it, Darren replied, 'Yeah, sorry I'm flat out at the minute, it won't happen again' but it did happen again, and maybe again after that, then it's time to turn up the dial and bring a little more—as Raymond puts it—heat to the situation.

Step 2: The invitation

Once we've observed the same undesirable behaviour two to three more times, then it's time for the invitation, which sounds like:

'Hey Darren, so you know I mentioned the agenda a couple of weeks ago. Well I've noticed there have been two or three more times where you've not been ready for the meeting. Is there anything you'd like to chat about? Anything I can help you with?'

Again, notice the language. Turning up the heat doesn't mean turning down the care. We're not become more punitive as we move through the dial; we're becoming more deliberate about wanting to talk about the issue.

During the mention, it was, 'Is everything alright?' We turn up the heat, while still caring, and avoiding blame, judgement or shame by asking, 'Is there anything you'd like to chat about? Anything I can help you with?'

Again, the option here is for Darren to commit to improving or discuss with you what's causing the issue. And again, at Utopia Inc. from that day on Darren always read his agenda.

But of course, in the real world he didn't. In which case it's time for step 3 in the Dial, the conversation, and notice how Raymond doesn't call this the 'difficult conversation' because, put simply, it doesn't need to be. It's at this point that the SHIFT Conversation, with a little tweak, can be repurposed nicely here.

Step 3: The conversation

You've used the mention and the invitation and Darren is still not adequately preparing for meetings, and it's having an impact on the team and their ability to be effective. In steps 1 and 2 you asked if Darren would like to talk about the issue. In step 3, you turn up the heat by insisting you talk about the issue. However, again, you're high on the care factor. You're still not bringing blame, judgement or shame into the mix. You're also being very mindful of what you're bringing to the table:

- Are you using Blue mind?

- Have you left your biases at the door?

- Are you ready to be present and curious?

I also want you to consider:

- Can you resist the urge to 'win' the conversation?

- Can you not ask questions you already know the answer to?

- And can you not script the whole conversation?

I sometimes get push back on this last one, usually from people who have attended a 'How to have a difficult conversation' workshop.

They miss the irony that by having a script you're only making the conversations more difficult because

scripts are only useful if both parties have read them.

If Darren knows his lines, then great, use the script.

But I'm tipping he's got a different story to tell, so I'm going to listen with genuine curiosity to see what I might learn. All that said, I think it's useful to craft a specific opening in order to get into the conversation.

Identify when the most recent issue was:

'Last week in our team meeting ...'

State the issue:

'By not having your presentation ready ...'

State how it made you feel and a concern you have. Avoid speaking on behalf of others:

'I felt let down, and a bit disrespected to be honest. We've spoken about this a few times now, you've told me everything's okay and you've committed to turning up to our meetings fully prepared. And I am worried about how this might end up affecting the team.'

Ask a question you don't know the answer to:

'So I'm curious, what's your take on that?'

This opening forms the 'scan' of your SHIFT Conversation. From here, remain focused on the issue, but seek to establish what the real challenges are for Darren.

It's even more likely in these types of conversations that Darren will attempt to stay on the surface of challenges, so it's important to keep probing until you get a sense of what's really causing the problem.

Also, remember when you ask people what they want, they're quite likely to turn it back on you with things they want you to do. In this case you must always remember that 'No' is on the table, as in:

> **Darren:** 'I need you to take these three projects off my hands so I have more time.'

> **You:** 'No Darren, that isn't really an option. Do you think you can come up with an alternative, over which you have—at least—some control?'

By using the map for a SHIFT Conversation, you're able to navigate to a point where Darren commits to a new behaviour that addresses his issues around lack of preparedness, but instead of asking, 'When should I check in with you?' the heat is increased slightly by your asking instead, 'When are we likely to see this new behaviour?'

Darren sets the timeline, and this doesn't have to be a huge new way of being. It just needs to be a shift (see what I did there?) in the right direction.

Back at Utopia ... actually, scrap that. Back in the real world, deploying these three steps will significantly reduce drama in the workplace and the need for so-called 'difficult' conversations. The mention, invitation and conversation are all opportunities for Darren to say what he'll do, in the manner in which he'll do it, against agreed norms, and for the vast majority of people you work with, this works.

But let's say, for whatever reason, Darren still doesn't change. In that case we move to step 4, the boundary.

Step 4: The boundary

In my interpretation of the Accountability Dial, the heat gets turned up at step 4 like this:

'Hey Darren, you know you committed to doing X by this week? I haven't seen it. Do we need to rethink this? Because I need to see it by close of business next Tuesday at the absolute latest.'

If Darren does need another conversation, fine, but ensure you define when you need to see action.

In step 3, Darren sets the timeline. In step 4 you set it.

Step 5: The limit

The limit is the point at which there's nowhere left to go. If you're a middle leader, this is the point where you move the issue up the chain. If you're the big boss, this is probably the point where you move the person out of their current role, or perhaps out of the organisation altogether. But before you do that, you give it one last shot like this:

'Darren, I don't know what else to try. We've been working on this for several weeks/months now. I need you to go away over the weekend and have a think about whether or not there's something we can do, because you need to know, if there isn't an immediate and lasting improvement, we're out of options. It's going to mean you go on a performance management plan.'

Remember Sohail, who didn't like confrontation and didn't want to risk the relationships in his team? Well, I can report that his team have now all signed off on sets of norms for various aspects of their work. Furthermore, they—not Sohail—now hold each other accountable by using the mention and the invitation, and the need for what might previously have been called 'difficult' conversations has reduced. What's more, even when such a conversation is required, because of the work done in setting the norms and then deploying the mention and invitation, these conversations tend to be far more positive than they are difficult.

These approaches lead to less difficult conversations both in number and feel.

Is there a conversation you know you need to have but you're hoping not to have?

It might be with someone you work with, a close friend, or perhaps someone you live with, and they're doing something that you don't agree with. It might be something minor, but it grinds your gears, and while you're able to tolerate it for the moment, it's far from ideal. Or, it might be something quite significant. It could be that someone is engaging in unethical, illegal or self-destructive behaviour, and even though you care for them, you don't say anything. Or is it because you do care for them that you don't say anything because you don't want to damage your relationship? Do you hope that things will sort themselves out, or they'll just realise what they're doing and stop?

I ask again, is there a conversation you know you need to have but you're hoping not to?

....

....

....

....

What's stopping you?

....

....

....

....

How might you use the 'Is it Acceptable?' activity, the Accountability Dial and the SHIFT Conversation to approach things in future?

....

....

....

....

The sweet spot

After reading this chapter:

What new insight(s) do you have?

....

....

....

....

What new intention(s) do you have?

....

....

....

....

What action(s) will you start / stop / keep doing in order to enhance your leadership?

....

....

....

....

CONCLUSION

Roger Federer still feels the need for a coach, and you don't? Seriously?

This conclusion in a nutshell

- you'll be encouraged to reflect on the insights this book has provided for you

- you'll be encouraged to enlist a coach or trusted colleague in your leadership development

- you'll have the opportunity to 'coach yourself' by completing the final reflection questions

This entire book has been an attempt to coach you towards being the leader you really want to be. I want to close it out by being somewhat direct in this attempt.

Remember my coaching philosophy relies on helping the people I work with cycle through this process.

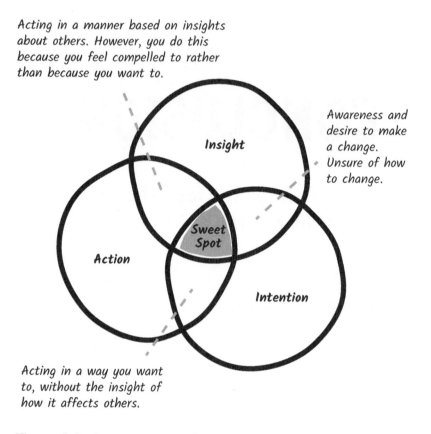

Acting in a manner based on insights about others. However, you do this because you feel compelled to rather than because you want to.

Insight

Awareness and desire to make a change. Unsure of how to change.

Sweet Spot

Action

Intention

Acting in a way you want to, without the insight of how it affects others.

Figure C.1: the sweet spot of coaching

Through the various chapters, I've tried to help you develop new ways of thinking, being and acting in your role as a leader.

For this book to achieve what I hoped it would achieve when I set out writing it, it's imperative that something happens. It's imperative that something changes. (Unless of course you've determined nothing has to change.)

And this is where things get hard. Because change is hard. Talking about change is easy. For example, setting a New Year's resolution is easy. What's difficult is keeping it.

We would be more able to make changes if we did these three things:

- appreciate the nature of change

- set better goals

- stop relying on willpower alone.

And this is where enlisting a coach can be useful, as they are able to work side-by-side with you to navigate these three issues.

Depending on your context you may wish to hire a coach who has specific skills or knowledge relating to your domain. Or perhaps they have experience having 'been there and done that.' For example, an online search can direct you to business coaches, sales coaches, executive coaches, public speaking coaches and even parenting coaches. There are literally coaches for pretty much every human endeavour.

If you're brand new to a role, or just starting out, then having a coach who has some experience in that space can be beneficial. However, if you have been in your role for some time, then hiring a coach who doesn't have experience in your field presents a different set of opportunities for improvement.

It seems counter-intuitive, but hiring a coach who hasn't 'been there and done that' in your field means that the nature of the relationship is significantly different.

Imagine for a second that you're working with a coach who you know was very successful in a similar role to yours. When they ask you, 'So tell me, why are you doing that?,' your response is likely to be influenced by one of two thoughts ...

- *Thought #1*: 'Sh!t, why? What *should* I be doing?'

- *Thought #2*: 'C'mon, you've been in this role, you *know* why we're doing that.'

But if you're working with someone you know doesn't have experience in your role, when they ask, 'So tell me, why are you doing that?,' you are more likely to explain what you're doing. If the coach is using my SHIFT model, this would likely be part of the Scan.

I've never run an ASX-listed company, played in the National Rugby League, or been a principal of a school. I've never headed up a national sales team, represented Australia at the Olympics or been the father of twins who don't speak to him. And yet, by applying the thinking in this book, I been able to help them improve.

That's what a coach can do. They can't tell you what to do and then consider their work done. And they can't do the work for you. But what they can do is help you to navigate change so that you don't view setbacks, or detours, as failure, or as evidence you can't change.

They can help you set better goals, because they have an objective view of your situation, and a suite of tools to help elicit the outcomes you truly want to achieve; not just the ones you *think* you're capable of or – worse – the goals you feel compelled to achieve to appease or please others.

And a good coach will give you strategies to help stay accountable. They will help you establish what is within your control and what falls outside, and then help you direct your time, energy and effort on the former, while helping you to let go of the latter. When you have a good coach, they're not there to act as your personal cheerleader, but you know that they will have your back. They are there to help you develop a new awareness, to help you clarify your intentions and to create new actions in order for you be the professional, partner, parent, person you want or need to be.

This takes a degree of vulnerability on your part. You have to be open to change.

Of course — as a coach — I'd urge you to explore this. But if you're not ready yet, that is fine too.

Coaching isn't for everyone.
Until they realise it is.

So, for now, let's explore how you might start coaching yourself by better understanding change, setting better goals, and reducing our reliance on willpower.

Let's tackle each in turn, and then come up with a system to give us a better chance of change.

Appreciate the nature of change

Change is not just a case of one day you're not doing something and the next day you decide to do something and then for the rest of your days you keep doing that thing.

Rather, there's a lot of nuance and a number of factors that go into whether or not you're able to change. I've found a particular model of change to be really useful when I'm working with athletes or leaders in order to locate where they are with regard to a specific change attempt. It's called the Transtheoretical Model of Change (boring name—great model!).

This model of change originated in the healthcare system, and we're going to use your health as a way of illustrating the nature of change, how to set better goals and how to rely on more than just willpower.

Once we've done that, you'll be able to apply this to a change you'd like to make as a result of reading this book.

Stage 1: blissfully unaware

The first stage of change is what's referred to as *the pre-contemplative stage of change*. At this stage of change we're blissfully unaware of the need to change. We're living our life thinking everything's fine.

We don't consider that we might need to change anything in order to improve our health.

To be clear, every single one of us, right, now is in the pre-contemplative stage of change with regard to something we're going to have to address down the track—for one form of change or another. There's something right now that we're blissfully unaware of that needs to change.

Stage 2: stop and think

However, there's usually a moment that moves us from the pre-contemplation stage of change into the next stage of change, and that moment could be as simple as playing basketball with your son and finding yourself shocked at how short of breath you are; or perhaps it's a photograph from an unflattering angle; or perhaps you go to the doctor and get blood test results that aren't too serious, but there's something there that's started to make you think. And that's when you move into *the contemplation stage of change.*

As the word suggests, we start contemplating the need for change. We stop and think, and this could be compounded by comments from others. It might be your son making fun of you getting out of breath or your doctor saying, 'Hey, these results are suggesting that you might want to think about cutting down on your salt intake or reducing your alcohol consumption or perhaps you want to think about getting more exercise'.

From this point on, we're no longer blissfully unaware of the need for change. We're now aware, and we're thinking about it. We start weighing up the pros and cons of making a change. Of course, we know the benefit of reducing our alcohol intake. We know the benefit of taking exercise or reducing our cholesterol levels and we know that in all likelihood, doing these things will lead to a longer, more productive, healthier life. Not only will we get to see our kids grow up, but hopefully our kids' kids grow up.

The benefits to living a healthier life are obvious, but the costs of living a healthier life are often equally obvious. Perhaps you like a beer and don't want to cut down on that. Perhaps you've never enjoyed exercise because of your schooling experience with a sadistic gym teacher or maybe you don't like the idea of cutting down on your red meat intake. Smoking is an excellent example of this. There isn't a single person who isn't aware of the health dangers associated with smoking, but the cons or the costs to that person of giving up smoking are 'Well, I enjoy it. I like it'. And they'll tell you that it relieves their stress or they only smoke to be social.

In many scenarios, the contemplation phase is often as far as we get. That's why, when you ask people, 'Do you exercise?' or 'Have you thought about cutting down on alcohol?' they say, 'Yeah, yeah, I thought about it. It's just not for me'. They stay in that contemplation phase. They can never go back to being blissfully unaware. They can never go back to not knowing that their alcohol consumption, their salt intake, their red meat intake is an issue. They now know that their alcohol consumption or diet is an issue; it's just that—for whatever reason—they don't do anything about it.

They can never go back there. They stay in the contemplation phase because, at that point, the cons have outweighed the pros of making that change.

Stage 3: Ready ... set ...

And that's why, unfortunately, it often takes a major event for people to move from the contemplation phase into *the preparation phase of change*, which is the third phase. It takes a significant health scare. Not just the doctor suggesting you think about something, but for some people it may take a heart attack for them to actually be proactive with regard to their health. Whether it's taken a major life event or not (hopefully not!) for you to move from the contemplation to the preparation phase, it's here that you're clear that there's something you want to do. So here you get ready. You set yourself up for the new behaviour.

For example, if you've decided to exercise more, preparation could include looking around the local area for different gyms and researching the different membership options. Or perhaps it's a trip to the shops to buy a new exercise outfit and get fitted for some good running shoes. It could be finding a friend who you could go for a walk with. You put all these things in place, which will help you to act.

Another form of preparation in this phase is mental preparation. If you've decided you're going to cut down on your alcohol consumption to only drink on weekends or at big events such as birthdays or the like, you might need to mentally prepare to not drink. You might need to be prepared to say, 'No thanks' when you're offered a drink at a party or when you're out for a meal.

I can't overstate the importance of this phase because without properly preparing, when we move into the next phase, which is *the action phase of change*, we either don't follow through and do as well as we might or it's only a very short term new behaviour.

Stage 4: Just do it!

The action phase is when you finally do it. You go to the gym. You refuse a beer after work, opting instead for a ginger ale.

Congratulations. You're a changed person!

Except you're not ...

Doing something new once is relatively easy. Continuing to do something new is hard.

That's why fitness gyms can continually sign up new members. They know they won't keep coming. Imagine if they did! Imagine if everybody who joined the gym actually went to the gym regularly. There would be no room at the gym. But gym owners are well aware that the vast majority of their members buy a gym membership, start off well, then their visits become less regular until at some point they stop going. They'll keep paying for the gym membership, they just won't use it.

Which leads us to the fork in the road of the change model. After doing something in the action phase, we either move into *the maintenance phase*, where it stops being a 'new' behaviour and becomes a norm, or usual behaviour. Or we *lapse*. When we lapse, we can lapse back into any of the stages of change other than the pre-contemplative stage. We can never again be blissfully unaware of the need to change. But we might lapse back to the contemplation stage, and think about it some more, to come up with some different strategies to address our health or settle on a decision not to do anything. We might lapse back to the preparation stage and conduct more research about our strategies because the preparation we'd done previously didn't take into account all the other factors in our life. Or we might lapse back into the action phase by trying something else for the first time.

Figure C.2 is a simple illustration of the stages of change.

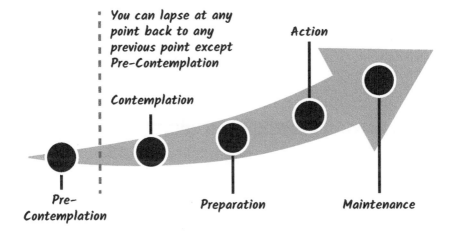

Figure C.2: the stages of change

Set better goals

When we think of goal setting, it's not unusual for people to immediately think of SMART goals, and while this theory of goal-setting has its place, I like to help people articulate their goals by asking these questions:

- What's the big vision here? What are you aiming for?

- What will you be able to do that indicates you're getting closer to achieving this? We call these performance goals.

- What new habits will you need in order to do these things? We call these process goals.

We then draw it out as shown in figure C.3.

We then reflect each week with regard to these process habits.

Did we achieve our process goals as often as we had planned to that week? If the answer is 'yes', then that's great. We might decide whether we should keep the same process goals for the next week, or tweak them a little. But if the answer is, 'No, I wasn't able to achieve my process goals this week', this is when we discuss the nature of the lapse. Was it a case of poor preparation? Was it because you weren't feeling well? Was it because something came up at work? Was it because you never really wanted to do it in the first place—you just felt compelled to?

Stop relying on willpower alone

There are so many factors that mean it might be harder to make a change than you originally thought, so relying on willpower alone is limiting your chances of successfully making a change. Of course, willpower is important, but being able to enlist others in your initiative is crucial. Having someone to talk to about why you've lapsed can encourage a renewed attempt, whereas if left to your own devices to stew on your setbacks—remember the ANTs in chapter 4?—it's likely that this might go down as another thing you tried once.

For example, in the scenario above, if you don't achieve your process goals for any one of those reasons, your confidence to achieve might be dented and as a result willpower can be diminished. This is especially true if you've held a fixed mindset towards the new

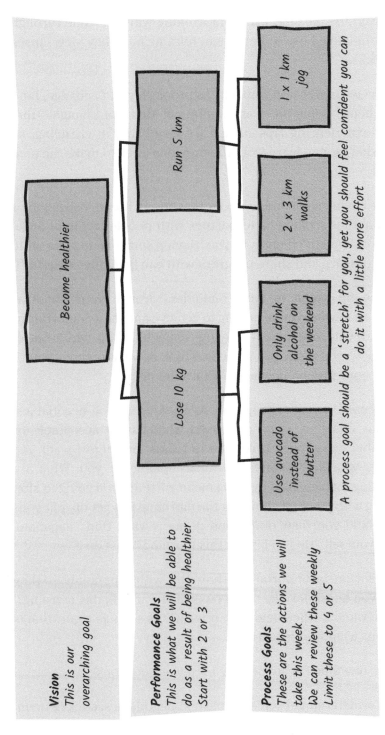

Figure C.3: goal tree

behaviour in the past. So when I'm working with someone through a change initiative I like to help them reframe how they view lapses and setbacks.

Many perceive lapses and setbacks as proof they can't change, but I put it to them—using the Transtheoretical Model of Change—that if they're experiencing lapses then it's proof they're changing, so let's see what we can learn from the previous week to make the next one better.

As well as having someone to check in with—a friend, colleague or coach—another strategy is to partner with people trying to make the same, or similar, changes to you. Having someone to train with, walk with or learn and share progress with can be really powerful.

It can also be useful to have reminders around your home or workplace as to what you're hoping to achieve and more importantly, why you're trying to achieve it. Staying connected to the why is one of the most powerful strategies there is. Think how many times you've heard someone give up because, 'What's the point?'

Staying focused increases willpower. As does having non-negotiables. In previous chapters we've discussed what having acceptable or unacceptable behaviours looks like in teams, but here I want you to consider what's acceptable and unacceptable for you. What are your non-negotiables? And by this I mean what are you going to stop negotiating with yourself about? In the morning, just get up, put your shoes on (and your new outfit) and go for a walk. Don't negotiate. Don't ask yourself, 'Do I feel like it this morning?' Just do it.

Sometimes it can be important to share this with your family, so they don't ask you questions like, 'Are you going for a walk this morning?' or 'Do you want a coffee before your walk?' As soon as a question is posed, your willpower is tested.

This is the one time I'm advocating for fewer questions!

Once you've determined some simple non-negotiables, stick to them.

The Act of Leadership: What's going to change for you?

Using the 12 sweet spots you identified in the chapters of this book, answer these questions.

1. As a result of reading this book, what new insight(s) do you now have?

....

....

....

....

2. As a result of your new insight(s), what new intention(s) do you now have?

....

....

....

....

3. As a result of your new insight(s) and intention(s), what do you now want to do?

....

....

....

....

4. What does this look like as a goal tree? Use Figure C.4
    to create your own.

    ....

    ....

    ....

    ....

5. What are your non-negotiables?

    ....

    ....

    ....

6. Who will you enlist to support you in this? What will you
    need from them?

    ....

    ....

    ....

    ....

You skimmed all those questions didn't you?

You don't have time for them?

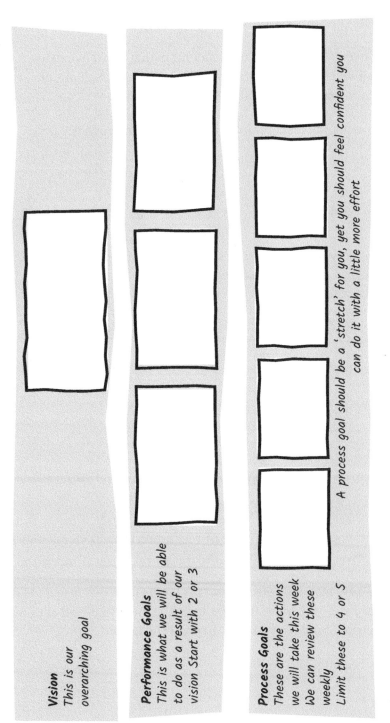

Figure C.4: goal tree template

Fair enough. Then answer these two questions to get the ball rolling:

1. Choose one aspect of your leadership that you'd like to, or you know you need to, improve and score yourself out of 10 with regard to your ability in that domain.

   The aspect of leadership I want / need to improve is:

   ....

   Score out of 10:   1   2   3   4   5   6   7   8   9   10

2. What do you need to do or stop doing in order to help yourself increase that score by 1?

   ....

   ....

   ....

   ....

Now you have a starting point at least.

Don't forget, you can grab a heap of resources to help you achieve success at www.actofleadership.com.

You can also get in touch with me and my team via the website and I'd love to hear from you about the new insights, intentions and actions that have come about for you as a result of the book.

Thanks for reading, and good luck!

Dan Haesler

ACKNOWLEDGEMENTS

First and foremost I need to thank my family: my wife Samira, and children Jackson and Harper. For the past decade I've been working with people all over Australia, the Asia–Pacific and even Europe. That means flights and nights away from home. Lots of them. It's this work that has informed every line in this book. Without their support and crucially their understanding, I'd never have written it. Samira was forthright in her feedback on the very first draft of the manuscript: 'Well, it's starting to get better ...' she told me after reading chapter 5.

Samira is also a director at Cut Through, and has supported me every step of the way—from the decision I made to leave a perfectly good, well-paying job to set up a new business whilst paying a mortgage in Sydney with two kids under three. No stress! ☺ Seriously though, Samira is the glue that holds our family and our professional world together. Love ya! x

To my parents back in the UK: I really appreciate the support, interest and enthusiasm you show during our weekly chats for whatever I'm up to, and I'm forever grateful for the work ethic you instilled in me growing up. Thank you.

I recognise that my work is built on the shoulders of giants, some of whom were gracious enough to share their time and thinking with me for my *Habits of Leadership* podcast, and in turn as part of this book. In particular, I'd like to thank Professor Richard Ryan, Professor Amy Edmondson, Professor Carol Dweck, Daniel Pink and Jonathan Raymond. It was also a real treat to be able to sit and chat with four-time Olympian Anna Meares and Australian Rugby League player Chris Lawrence.

Thank you to the team at Cut Through who, alongside Samira and me, drive our work. In particular, I'd like to thank Tim Perkins who, after Samira, was one of the first to read the manuscript and give me some excellent feedback before I sent it through to the publishers.

Thanks to Lucy Raymond and Frankie Tarquinio at Wiley for believing in the premise of the book right from the outset, to the editorial team of Chris Shorten, Sandra Balonyi and Ingrid Bond for helping craft it into the book it's become and to Marie-Anna Sultani and Renee Aurish in the marketing team for getting the word out and getting the book into many hands. Thank you!

And last (but certainly not least), thank you to you for deciding to spend your time reading this book. I sincerely hope you find the strategies and ideas in it helpful in order to help you and your people to thrive, professionally and personally.

INDEX

Printed and bound by CPI Group (UK) Ltd, Croydon, CR0 4YY
21/07/2021
03076916-0001